T0325290

Telling Terror in Judges 19

Telling Terror in Judges 19 explores the value of performing a 'reparative reading' of the terror-filled story of the Levite's *pilegesh* (commonly referred to as the Levite's concubine) in Judges 19 and how such a reparative reading can be brought to bear upon elements of modern rape culture. Historically, the story has been used as a morality tale to warn young women about what constitutes appropriate behaviour. More recently, (mainly male) commentators have tended to write the woman out of the story by making claims about its purpose and theme which bear no relation to her suffering. In response to this, feminist critics have attempted to write the woman back into the story, generally using the hermeneutics of suspicion. This book begins by surveying some of the traditional commentators and the three great feminist commentators of the text (Bal, Exum, and Trible). It then offers a reparative reading by attending to the surprising prominence of the *pilegesh*, her moral and marital agency, and her speaking voice. In the final chapter, there is a detailed comparison of the story with elements of modern rape culture.

Helen Paynter is a Baptist minister, Director of the Centre for the Study of Bible and Violence, and a tutor at Bristol Baptist College, UK.

Rape Culture, Religion and the Bible

Series Editors:

Katie Edwards
University of Sheffield, UK

Caroline Anne Blyth
University of Auckland, New Zealand

Johanna Stiebert
University of Leeds, UK

Rape Myths, the Bible and #MeToo
Johanna Stiebert

Telling Terror in Judges 19: Rape and Reparation for the Levite's Wife
Helen Paynter

For more information about this series, please visit: www.routledge.com/Rape-Culture-Religion-and-the-Bible/book-series/RCRB

Telling Terror in Judges 19

Rape and Reparation for the
Levite's Wife

Helen Paynter

Routledge
Taylor & Francis Group

LONDON AND NEW YORK

First published 2020
by Routledge
2 Park Square, Milton Park, Abingdon, Oxon OX14 4RN

and by Routledge
52 Vanderbilt Avenue, New York, NY 10017

Routledge is an imprint of the Taylor & Francis Group, an informa business

British Library Cataloguing-in-Publication Data
A catalogue record for this book is available from the British Library

Library of Congress Cataloging-in-Publication Data
A catalog record for this book has been requested

ISBN: 978-0-367-86088-2 (hbk)
ISBN: 978-1-003-01682-3 (ebk)

Typeset in Bembo
by Apex CoVantage, LLC

Contents

Acknowledgements and dedication

No book is ever written in isolation, and this is no exception. Ideas begin to germinate when reading the work of scholars who have gone before; we enter a conversation that started long before we put pen to paper. The growing thought is fed by conversations, formal and informal. I speak at various events and often take questions which set hares running in my mind. Students make comments in seminars. I try out ideas on my colleagues and friends at Bristol Baptist College. I read the newspapers and watch my Twitter feed. It is impossible to cite every influence that shapes an idea, although I have obviously referenced every one that seemed significant. But I am grateful for them all.

One of the big influences in shaping my thinking for this book was the Shiloh conference on Religion and Rape Culture, held in Sheffield in July 2018. I travelled up from Bristol with three bright students and we all found the event highly stimulating. The ideas for this book were already in my mind at that time, but they were sharpened and shaped by several of the papers presented that day. I am grateful to all the fantastic scholars who run the Shiloh Project, and to the speakers for their stimulation to my thinking. I am delighted that this book will be part of the Shiloh Project's 'Rape Culture, Religion and the Bible' series.

Of course, my thanks as always go to my family, who not only let me try out ideas on them (and some of these make for very poor dinner-time conversation) but also cheer me on continually. My love and gratitude go to my wonderful husband Stephen, who reads and comments with discernment on everything I write. My grateful love, too, to our elder daughters Susanna and Louisa, both away at university, and our youngest, Victoria, who has the misfortune to be home alone with us now. And my love and thanks to my father for all his support.

On the Sunday after the Shiloh conference, I preached a sermon about rape, pornography, and sexual abuse at the church I was then minister of. After that service, four individuals told me about their own experiences of sexual assault. I was heart-broken.

This book is dedicated to you and all the other people
I know who have experienced sexual assault. I may not
know who you all are, but God does.

It is also dedicated to the memory of Beli-Fachad and
Jyoti Singh ('Nirbhaya') who endured what no one
should ever have to.

And finally, it is dedicated to the memory of my
mother, Eleanor Batchelor, who died while I was
writing this book. I miss you more than I can say.
Until we meet again.

Introduction

The story in Judges 19 of the rape and murder of the Levite's *pilegesh* (פִּילֶגֶשׁ), often referred to as his concubine,[1] has puzzled, enraged, and disturbed its readers for centuries. It is, in essence, an ancient narrative of a brutal act of sexual violence. It has, at different times, been interpreted in ways which centre the focus upon the woman's suffering and in ways which disregard her altogether. Historically, it has at times been deployed as a cautionary tale against female sexual infidelity, and the woman's fate has sometimes been attributed to her own sin. Modern readers, particularly feminist critics, tend to draw attention to these misogynistic readings which it has inspired and accuse the text itself of inherent misogyny. Are its detractors right that the only way to read it in the 21st century is with a hermeneutic of suspicion? Or are there more positive ways of engaging with this narrative? Might it have something constructive to say to us?

The story is one which refuses to stay on the page. It has, as we shall see, a visceral effect upon the reader. It also has many points of similarity with modern situations of sexual violence, particularly sexual violence against women. In the first part of this monograph, we will briefly set out the account of the Levite's *pilegesh*. We will next go on to survey some of the history of interpretation of this story, first considering earlier interpreters, who have traditionally decentred the woman's suffering, and then turning to modern feminist readings, which tend towards a suspicious hermeneutic. We will then offer an alternative reading, inspired by Eve Sedgwick's call for a 'reparative reading' of texts.

Sedgwick's starting point is that 'for someone to have an unmysti-fied, angry view of large and genuinely systemic oppressions does not *intrinsically* or *necessarily* enjoin on that person any specific train of epistemological or narrative consequences.' She argues that merit can be sought within the text; good surprises rather than hostile ones. We will therefore consider whether a reparative hermeneutic enables us to view this text without suspicion but still without misogyny.

Although she does not use the precise term, Susan Brownmiller probably originated the idea of 'rape culture' in her highly influen-tial book *Against Our Will*, published in 1975. She describes how the existence of certain norms and attitudes within society com-bine to constitute a culture which condones and facilitates rape.

> [T]hese attitudes, [. . .] offer men, and in particular, impres-sionable, adolescent males, who form the potential raping population, the ideology and psychologic encouragement to commit their acts of aggression without awareness, for the most part, that they have committed a punishable crime, let alone a moral wrong. The myth of the heroic rapist that permeates false notions of masculinity, from the success-ful seducer to the man who 'takes what he wants when he wants it,' is inculcated in young boys from the time they first become aware that being a male means access to certain mysterious rites and privileges, including the right to buy a woman's body. When young men learn that females may be bought for a price, and that acts of sex command set prices, then how should they not also conclude that that which may be bought may also be taken without the civility of a monetary exchange?[2]

Typical of rape culture is a set of attitudes which objectify women, minimise the value of women as humans, and seeks to control their sexuality.[3] These values are sustained by a mesh of 'rape myths,' which are prejudiced, stereotyped, and false beliefs about the victims and perpetrators of rape.[4] If rape culture is under-stood in this way, then it is undeniable that the society within which Judges 19 is set shows such elements, even though the term itself is anachronistic. Whether the narrator himself (for he surely is a 'he') is accepting of rape culture is a question that will be addressed throughout. I shall argue that in many important respects he distantiates himself from the uncritical norms of the society he is describing.

More disturbingly, as we shall see, traditional scholarship that engages with this narrative has shown itself to be uncritically accepting of certain elements of rape culture. It is the purpose of this work to investigate whether a reparative reading of the narrative can resist such an uncritical compliance with these norms and thereby be redemptive for modern readers, particularly those who have experienced serious sexual assault.[5]

The investigation will be based upon the final form of the text,[6] with sensitivity to the ancient context in which the story is set. It will use a narrative approach, seeking to identify the textual indicators which suggest the features the author is intending to foreground. It will look, in particular, at the question of the voice and agency of the *pilegesh*. Is she simply 'acted upon,' as is conventionally described? I will argue that close attention to the layers of communication within the text reveal that she has subjectivity within most of them.

I have written elsewhere of the need for biblical violence to be treated with a 'thick description,' which uses insights gained by a wide variety of interpretive lenses.[7] In response to my own imperative, then, the study which follows makes use of feminist theory, critical theories, speech act theory, affect theory, and Judith Butler's concept of grievability. It will seek to bring these into dialogue with one another and with traditional and feminist commentators, in the pursuit of a reading of this dreadful story which brings redemption.

Finally, a note about the naming convention I have adopted. Some authors have named the *pilegesh*; Exum chooses 'Bath-Sheber' and Bal uses 'Beth.'[8] Although, as I will argue, the anonymity of the woman is not inherently an objectifying action on the part of the narrator, it seems to me as a modern writer that it esteems her dignity if she is given a name in this work. I have chosen, then, to call her Beli-Fachad, which is Hebrew for 'Fearless One.'[9]

Notes

1 The designation of the woman as 'concubine' has been used to validate the violence against her, and therefore in this paper I will use the untranslated term *pilegesh*.

2 Susan Brownmiller, *Against Our Will: Men, Women, and Rape* (New York: Ballantine Books, 1993), 391.

3 Yumi Suzuki, "Rape: Theories of," in *The Encyclopedia of Theoretical Criminology* (Hoboken: Wiley and Sons, 2014), 703–5.

4 Martha R. Burt, "Cultural Myths and Supports for Rape," *Journal of Personality and Social Psychology* 38, no. 2 (1980): 217–30, 217.

5 This has previously been explored by Susanne Scholz in *Sacred Witness: Rape in the Hebrew Bible* (Minneapolis: Fortress, 2010). Scholz's concern is to read the combined witness of the biblical rape texts alongside modern feminist perspectives on rape, and thereby offer a 'hermeneutic of meaning' as a supplement to the more familiar hermeneutic of suspicion. Scholz deals with the Levite's *pilegesh* on pages 139–50.

6 Except where indicated, translations are the author's own.

7 Helen Paynter, "Towards a Thick Description of Biblical Violence," in *Proceedings of the First Academic Symposium of the Centre for the Study of Bible and Violence*, ed. H Paynter and M. Spalione (Sheffield: Sheffield Phoenix, forthcoming).

8 Exum's choice of 'Bath-Sheber' (daughter of breaking) is made to mirror 'Bathsheba,' with whom the woman's story is compared; to reflect the woman's personal anguish and brokenness of spirit; and to signify the feminist critic's role in breaking open the text to reveal its phallocentric ideology. Cheryl Exum, *Fragmented Women: Feminist (Sub)versions of Biblical Narratives JSOT Suppl. 163* (Sheffield: Sheffield Academic Press, 1993), 176–77.

Beth is the Hebrew for 'house.' Bal chooses this name as she considers the woman to be defined by the location of her married life (in her father's house or her husband's). Mieke Bal, *Death and Dissymmetry: The Politics of Coherence in the Book of Judges* (Chicago: University of Chicago Press, 1988), 90.

9 My choice will be explained further in Chapter 5.

1 Beli-Fachad in the hands of men

Readers unfamiliar with the story of the Levite's *pilegesh* should put this book down and read the text (ideally in Hebrew) before proceeding; it speaks better for itself than I can. A brief summary, however, is offered here, without the intention of foreclosing the subsequent discussion.

A Levite marries a second wife, or takes a concubine,[1] who is from Bethlehem in Judah. For reasons which are unclear (we will discuss this later), she leaves him and returns home to her father. After four months, the Levite decides to try to bring her home. (Why the delay? The text is mute. Perhaps he is dilatory in his interest in the woman. Perhaps he has to attend to pressing matters at home, such as a harvest. Perhaps he wishes to discern whether or not she is pregnant.)

Whatever the reason for the delay, the Levite eventually travels to Bethlehem to 'speak to her heart' – not to be understood as an appeal to her affection so much as an appeal to her reason. He is welcomed by the woman's father; the woman herself is entirely out of our sight at this point. For four long days, and a substantial portion of the story (seven out of thirty verses), the father delays the Levite's departure with lavish hospitality. Is he simply a generous host, or is he reluctant to let the couple go on their way? And if so, why? We are not told. Eventually, and far too late on the fifth day, the Levite insists, and sets out with the *pilegesh* and his servant.

As night approaches, they are near a Canaanite town called Jebus. (This will later be conquered and renamed Jerusalem.) Rather than seek shelter in a foreign place, the Levite insists that they continue a little further, and they end up in the Israelite town of Gibeah at sundown. Here, in contrast with the lavish hospitality of the father-in-law, they are not welcomed. They linger in the town square, expecting an invitation to rest for the night but not receiving one. Eventually an old man comes along, not himself a native of the city but a resident alien from the hill country of Ephraim (the Levite's home turf). The old man takes them into his home, and they make merry (Hebrew: 'their hearts were good').

Suddenly there is a pounding on the door. A group of local thugs, 'sons of Belial,' have surrounded the house, and are demanding that the Levite be sent out to them so that they can 'know' (ידע) him. The hostile nature of the engagement and the subsequent use of the same word in the assault on the woman (v.25) makes it clear that they are not seeking to make his acquaintance but to rape him.[2] The host remonstrates with them, offering his own virgin daughter and the *pilegesh* in the Levite's stead. The offer is not well received, but eventually the man (we infer this is the Levite due to the affixed possessive pronoun) seizes his *pilegesh* – the virgin daughter has disappeared from the scene – and puts her out to the mob. Then 'they know her and abuse her until morning.' She survives the night and makes her way back to the house where her husband/master is sheltering. Is she denied admittance, or are they all asleep? We are only told that she falls at the door, her hands upon the threshold.

Morning comes, and the Levite is ready to continue his journey. He opens the door, steps over his woman (or so the story would seem to imply), saying just two words to her in Hebrew, 'Get up! Let's go.' There is no answer. Is she dead, or has she simply passed out? We are not told.[3] He puts her on his donkey and completes his journey. When he gets home, he takes a knife, seizes the woman, and butchers her into twelve pieces. *Now* she is certainly dead.

The woman's dismembered body is sent around the towns of Israel as a military muster, in a similar fashion to the muster by Saul in 1 Samuel 11:7 – except that Saul uses a pair of oxen, not a bruised and bleeding wife.[4] As a result of the muster (we are straying into chapter 20), 'all the people of Israel' turn out in consternation. The Levite gives a highly selective account of the events leading to the woman's death, and the nation descends into civil war – not only civil war, but mass abduction of women and rape. We will not be working closely with chapters 20 and 21, but we will be following some of the threads of the *pilegesh*'s story into these concluding chapters.

Before we move on, we should notice the literary framing of the narrative. It begins with the words: 'In those days there was no king in Israel.' This is the first half of a *motif* repeated several times in Judges (17:6; 21:25; and in the shorter version as here, 18:1). The second half of the *motif* is found in verse 24, when the old man suggests that the mob may do to his daughter and the *pilegesh* 'what is good in your eyes.' The story, or this element of it, concludes (v.30) with Israel saying to itself: 'Apply yourselves to it. Take counsel. Speak.'

The use of the *Leitmotif* of Judges within this pericope alerts us to the centrality of this story within the purpose of the book.[5] Israel's self-exhortation reaches out of the text and addresses the reader. Apply yourself to it. Take counsel. Speak.

Let us do so.

Notes

1 The exact nature of a *pilegesh* is ambiguous, as will be discussed later.
2 ידע is frequently used of sexual knowledge, e.g. Gen 4:1; 1Kgs 1:4; Num 31:17.
3 We are not told in the Hebrew text. The Septuagint has an inserted phrase in verse 28: 'She did not answer him *for she had died*.'
4 Daniel Block points out that there is precedent for using a dismembered human body in the royal archives of Mari. 'To my lord, speak. Baḫdi-Lim your servant [speaks] as follows: For five full days I have waited for the Hanaeans but the people do not gather. The Hanaeans have arrived from the steppe and established themselves among the settlements. Once, twice, I have sent [word] to the settlements and the appeal has been made. But they have not gathered together, and for the third day they have not gathered. Now, if I had my way, a prisoner in jail should be killed, his body dismembered, and transported to the area between the villages as far as Hudnim and Appan in order that the people would fear and gather quickly, and I could make an attempt in accordance with the command which my lord has given, to carry out the campaign quickly.' Quoted in Daniel I. Block, *Judges, Ruth New American Commentary, Volume 6* (Nashville: Broadman & Holman Publishers, 1999), 546.
5 We will shortly consider scholarly views which disagree with this.

2   Beli-Fachad in the hands of commentators

Writing about biblical rape in its diverse manifestations, Susanne Scholz comments that

> The history of interpretation is so exhaustively filled with missed recognition of rape in the Hebrew Bible and, worse, misclassification of rape as seduction, marriage, or even love. The disconnection between the biblical literature and the history of interpretation could not be more drastic. It has also led to the absence of biblical rape texts from religious teaching, preaching, and learning.[1]

The gap between text and interpreter is very clear in the history of interpretation of Judges 19. Traditional interpretations have often glossed over Beli-Fachad's suffering or subordinated it to the larger concerns of men, based on what Mieke Bal calls a 'hierarchy of interests.'[2] At various times, this has been done in different ways: excision of the texts, decentring the *pilegesh*, or holding the woman responsible for her own fate. We will consider these one at a time before turning our attention to two significant feminist approaches to the text.

Traditional commentators

Excision of the chapters

Some have suggested that the final chapters of Judges form an appendix to the book proper. Thus, for example, Yairah Amit argues that the natural conclusion to the book is formed by chapters 17 and 18, and that chapters 19 onward are not a thematic sequel, but describe a 'deviant incident' which provides a pretext for the author to praise the coherence and effective functioning of the community.[3] Others have made the case that it is chapters 17–21 which form the appendix.[4] Such conclusions are not inevitable, however. Other scholars have provided evidence of literary and thematic coherence between Judges 19–21 and the remainder of the book.[5]

This is not a merely theoretical question. Mieke Bal points out that the excision of Judges 19–21 (or the more extensive excision of chapters17–21) erases the most potent 'female' story in the whole text. While other narratives about women remain after such excision, the argument that the book of Judges is 'about' male concerns then becomes much easier to sustain. She argues, therefore, that such a decision stems from its own ideological presupposition, which it feeds in turn.

> 'History' in the narrow sense of the narration of military, economic, and political change prevents scholars from seeing other issues and continuous structures. Among the biases that obscure a comprehensive understanding of the past is the tendency, close to ethnocentrism, to take the present as the starting point and norm. And, of course, androcentrism, the tendency to start from the central place of men in history and to consider the participation of women in history as an abnormality.[6]

Bal is identifying a circularity in the interpretive process. The text is declared to be 'about' male interests such as war, courage, and nationhood, and any texts which do not centre on these themes are then excluded from the main corpus by definition.

Even if the removal of these three chapters does not stem from ideological origins (conscious or subconscious), they have ideological consequences. If the final chapters are declared to be marginal, then their characters and their concerns are also marginalised. Thus, for example, Alberto Soggin refers insouciantly to chapters 17–21 as an 'appendix on various themes.'[7]

Decentring of the pilegesh

A second way in which interpreters have minimised attention upon Beli-Fachad is by offering interpretations and theological explanations for the events of Judges 19–21 which have little or no connection with her trauma.

Some commentators, particularly the earlier ones, focus upon the experience of her husband. So, for example, Denis the Carthusian, in the 15th century, considered the rape of the woman in place of her master to be the lesser of two evils:

> Here one could ask whether the old man should be excused from guilt for exposing or offering his own daughter and the Levite's wife to the lust of these impious men to avoid *a more serious crime*, namely the crime against nature.[8]

Writing around the turn of the 18th century, Matthew Henry reduced the atrocity to 'the domestic affairs' of the man:

> The three remaining chapters of this book contain a most tragical story of the wickedness of the men of Gibeah, patronised by the tribe of Benjamin, for which that tribe was severely chastised and almost entirely cut off by the rest of the tribes. [. . .] The domestic affairs of this Levite would not have been related thus largely but to make way for the following story of *the injuries done him*, in which the whole nation interested themselves.[9]

In similar vein, at the end of the 19th century, George Moore said:

> *The freemen of Gibeah attacked me* lit. *arose against me. – Me they meant to kill, and my concubine they* ravished *so that she died* [. . .] their purpose might very well be described as an attempt upon his life, especially since his concubine actually died under their maltreatment.[10]

This emphasis upon an averted 'homosexual' rape[11] rather than the actual rape is found in a modern publication by the conservative publishing house 'Day One.' In their study guide on Judges, Simon Robinson asks the following questions from people studying the passage:

> What were the similarities between the behaviour of the people of Israel and that of the citizens of Sodom and Gomorrah (see Gen. 19:1–11)?
> How does their behaviour conflict with the commands set out in Leviticus 18:22 and 20:13?
> In what ways are these practices a sign of God's judgement (see Rom. 1:24–32)?[12]

The Leviticus and Romans texts to which Robinson refers are about homosexual activity, thus centring and prioritising the 'homosexual' element of this story.

Similar is the argument of Daniel Block, who appears to accept uncritically the host's implicit assertion that 'homosexual' rape exceeds 'heterosexual' rape in wickedness. Twice, Block rhetorically asks the question as to why the one is worse than the other, then answers it with reference to the greater biblical witness about heteronormativity and an appeal to heterosexual intercourse as the grounds of procreation and intimacy. Whatever one's view on whether the Bible is heteronormative, the idea that Beli-Fachad's rape could ever fulfil either of these functions is disturbing.[13]

Robinson also places a strong stress on the hospitality aspect of the story, an emphasis that is shared by Michael Wilcock.[14] Indeed, some commentators have gone so far as to say that it is 'all about hospitality.'[15]

Other commentators decentre the woman by failing to discuss her in other than very general terms. Alberto Soggin writes of the narratives somewhat dismissively:

> There can be no doubt that the first of the two narratives [Judges 19] seems somewhat irrelevant from the point of view of the historian and is, rather a literary 'novel'; furthermore the narrator has drawn considerably on Ge. 19, but without much coherence.[16]

Robert Boling manages to write three pages of comment on the story of Judges 19 without using a single female pronoun.[17] Indeed, his comment a couple of pages earlier, 'it was a man's world' (p. 274), seems curiously apt. His commentary on the events of the night has nothing to say about the rape, skipping straight from verse 25 to verse 28 (p. 276):

> 25. *The man seized his concubine.* Which man did this is not clear. It is probably the Levite, whose story is being told. Other protagonists – the father-in-law, the master of the house – are regularly identified by some such title.
> 28. *for she was dead.* With LXX, lost through haplography due to homoiou-teleuton in MT.

In a similar fashion, in his 1903 commentary, Robert Watson writes five pages on the episode containing only two female pronouns that might relate to the *pilegesh*.[18]

Finally, Adam Clarke smooths away the more horrific connotations of the passage for the benefit of his early 19th century audience by leaving them untranslated.

> vaiyedu othah, vaiyithallelu bah col hallailah, which we modestly translate, and they knew her, and they abused her all the night. More literally, but still not fully: Illi cum ea rem habuerunt, et alternatim in eam tota nocte ascenderunt. [. . .] The Arabic is not too strong; the following is its meaning: Exercuerunt in ea cupiditates suas, et mæchati, sunt in ea ad matutinum usque.[19]

Punishment interpretations

A different way of pushing the atrocity to the margins is to view it as just punishment for the woman's behaviour. The beginning of the story has the woman leaving her husband/master and returning to her father's house. The reason for her departure is unclear in the text. The Hebrew reads וַתִּזְנֶה עָלָיו פִּילַגְשׁוֹ. The verb זנה (zanah) refers to a woman's act of sexual impropriety, and may be employed to describe marital infidelity, fornication or prostitution; and by metaphorical extension is used of Israel's cultic infidelity. However, the best translation of the unique combination of verb and preposition זנה + על is unclear. Literally, it might be translated as 'whored upon,' and is therefore sometimes rendered 'played the harlot against him' (NASB) or 'played the whore against him' (AV).[20] The situation is complicated further, however, by the alternative version offered by the LXX, which has ὠργίσθη αὐτῷ ἡ παλλακὴ αὐτοῦ (his concubine became angry with him) which may have arisen from a textual error in the Hebrew where זנה (to commit sexual impropriety) and זנח (to reject) have become confused.[21]

Whichever version was in view, however, the early commentators frequently found occasion to criticise the woman's behaviour and thus to imply that her fate was her own fault. In Joy Schroeder's careful analysis of the use of these texts in Christian interpretation, *Dinah's Lament*, she assembles some striking examples of victim-blaming.[22]

Geoffroy de la Tour-Landry, writing in the 14th century, working on the basis that the *pilegesh* had abandoned her husband for no good reason, used the story as a salutary tale to warn his daughters about appropriate marital conduct. The woman's fate was the direct result of her 'leude ded' of leaving her husband, and her death was of shame not violence: 'on the morw, whanne she saye her self so shamed and defouled, she deyed for sorugh.'[23] Thus he draws the moral lesson:

> And therfor euery woman aught to restraine wrathe, and to plese and suffre her husbonde, and he be wroth, with faire langage, and not to go away from hym, as ded that woman, of the whiche come moche sorugh, as the dethe of her selff and of so gret nombre of pepill.[24]

The rediscovery of the Hebrew text, with its implication of adultery, led many of the reformers to the conclusion that the *pilegesh* was paying the price for her sins. Johannes Brenz, writing in 1535, says: 'By this heinous and abominable form of death our Lord God punished this woman's adultery. [. . .] God is not idle.'[25] The commentary of Martin Bucer, published in 1554, is of the same opinion:

> Here you see the woman's adultery finally punished by God, because her husband foolishly did not wish to punish her.

This, therefore, is the point: the adulterous woman, because she sinned through her own lust, paid, through the lust of another, a penalty more savage and shameful than the one prescribed by the law.[26]

Nor can such victim-shaming be entirely relegated to past generations. In his Bible handbook, published in 2009, Keith Brooks leaps to the brutal conclusion, 'in the miserable end of this woman, we see the hand of God punishing her for her uncleanness.'[27]

It is tempting to speculate whether the victim-blaming in which many commentators have indulged is plausible to them because their opinion of her character is coloured by their translation of *pilegesh* as 'concubine.' But the proper translation of this word here is unclear. As Trent Butler points out, the Levite has a חֹתֵן (father-in-law), implying a regularity about his relationship with Beli-Fachad.[28] Consider the description of Keturah, described by Genesis as Abraham's *isshah* (meaning woman, but commonly used for a wife, the same word used of Sarah),[29] but described by the Chronicler as a *pilegesh*.[30] Elsewhere *pilegesh* appears to be used in distinction to *isshah* (2 Samuel 5:13) and the offspring of a *pilegesh* are inferior in entitlement to the offspring of an *isshah* (1 Chronicles 3:19). So *pilegesh* sometimes means 'concubine,' but also appears to be used of a secondary wife; she does not share the status of a first wife.[31] Mieke Bal has developed this idea further, arguing that the term here relates to the wife in a patrilocal marriage (one in which the wife continues to reside with her father), and that in this text we can identify traces of the transition from this pattern of marriage to the new, virilocal style (in which the wife resides with her husband). This, Bal argues, explains the lengthy section at the beginning of the chapter where the *pilegesh*'s father appears loath to permit his daughter to return home with her husband.[32]

Although Bal's understanding of *pilegesh* has not been adopted in standard readings of the text, the very ambiguity about the exact meaning of the term might itself be considered to be symptomatic of a patriarchal society where a woman's status can be indicated with a single dismissive word, irrespective of whether she is a lawful wife, a concubine, or something else again. But it has also given license for generations of commentators to dismiss Beli-Fachad's ordeal as of little matter.

Feminist views

Notwithstanding all of this, if the *pilegesh* were a real, flesh-and-blood woman suffering in front of us, her plight would be very hard for even the most impervious of commentators to overlook. Perhaps it is because of this – for reason of the 'sticky affect' engendered by the woman's experience[33] – that the (male, in the main) commentators have skimmed over this story, or at least over the 'female' elements of it. The less real she becomes to us, the easier it is to overlook her plight and the less we are emotionally troubled by it. Or perhaps it is simply indifference and lack of imagination.

In response to these readings, and in the context of the rising tide of the hermeneutics of suspicion,[34] a new hermeneutical approach was applied to the text. From the late twentieth century onwards a slew of feminist scholars sought to identify and describe the abusive potential and effect of the text. Here we will consider two of the most influential: *Death and Dissymmetry* by Mieke Bal and *Raped by the Pen* by Cheryl Exum. The contribution of Phyllis Trible, the third giant in the field, will be considered a little later.

Mieke Bal: trapped in a patriarchal power struggle

In her provocative and deliberately unsettling book *Death and Dissymmetry: The Politics of Coherence in the Book of Judges*,[35] Mieke Bal uses an explicitly suspicious approach to the text, as well as to its previous interpreters.[36] But she does not want to obliterate the text. Instead, by anchoring it firmly into what she argues is its social setting (more firmly, she argues, than the traditional commentators), she seeks to uncover the deep-seated relationship between social institutions and violence against women.

At the very outset, Bal makes the perceptive observation that the deaths in Judges divide along gender lines. Male–upon–male deaths are military or political. (There are no female–upon–female killings.) Female–upon–male killings are also political: women kill military leaders and heroes. Male–upon–female killings are quite different: mighty men kill innocent defenceless women (pp. 1, 26ff). She views this as one example of the 'dissymmetry' of power with which the text is riddled. This dissymmetry is seen in terms of power over bodies, life, and language (p. 32).

Bal views Beli-Fachad (I will retain our name for the woman, for the sake of clarity) as trapped in a patriarchal system that incorporates both the text and its interpreters. Bal contests that there is a pathological circularity inherent within many interpreters' identification of the themes of the book. They decide that the book is 'about' male themes: the establishment of monotheism within the Promised Land, the political struggles of men, and the prequel to the failed kingship of Saul and the successful monarchy of David. This is the perceived 'coherence' of the book. Then, other elements of the book ('female' ones) which do not appear to support this coherence are subordinated in one way or another. We identified some examples of this in our previous discussion of the decentring of Beli-Fachad. However, Bal perceptively shows that the text itself is far more ambiguous than simply falling into 'male' and 'female' themes (p. 32). They often appear to be interpenetrated. So, domestic stories turn out to have political significance (for example, the giving of a bowl of curds to a fleeing military commander and covering him with a blanket, followed by his assassination), and military stories have domestic import (such as the murder of the daughter of Jephthah in exchange for his military victory).

One of the key themes of the book, as Bal sees it, is the ('female') theme of the tension between patrilocal (also called *beena*) and virilocal marriage. The traditional, patrilocal style of marriage in which the woman remained in her father's house and was visited periodically by her nomadic husband was being gradually replaced by the newer virilocal marriage in which the woman left her father's house to live in her husband's.[37] A wife who remains a daughter has her sexuality still under her father's control. Bal sees the power struggle between these two different ideologies within the first third of Judges 19, where Beli-Fachad's father appears reluctant to allow his son-in-law to take her away. Identifying this theme, rather than ignoring it in pursuit of a military-political 'coherence,' opens up for Bal the possibility of understanding Judges 19 in relation to the power structures that are at work. It uncovers an older, more drastic form of patriarchy, which is so dangerous that commentators have smoothed over the places in the text where it is hinted at. 'Such an awareness would begin to make the story really horrible' (p. 237). The woman is trapped between the two men who seek to assert their ownership of her.

This is related, as Bal constructs her argument, to the concept of 'virginity' within the book. Here Bal draws quite heavily upon the work of Sigmund Freud, who describes the male preoccupation with having a virgin bride as an expression of the male need to have a monopoly over her past (p. 52). Bal argues that there are two views of virginity within the text: the male and the female one (p. 72). For the woman, virginity is future-orientated; aiming towards the integration of her nobility into the whole life-cycle. In this sense, female virginity is threatening to men; a virgin is 'unknown' (because to have sexual intercourse is to 'know' a woman). For the man, virginity is about memory (a woman who comes to her first man with no 'history') and rapeability[38] (the potential of the nubile body). Hence the old man's offering of his virgin daughter and the *pilegesh* is not (in this sense) the offer of a virgin and an experienced woman, but the offer of two nubile, rapeable women.

So the events of the dreadful night, according to the counter-coherence which Bal offers, are (briefly) as follows. The Levite has won his power struggle with his father-in-law but has thereby transgressed the patrilocal pattern of marriage that is still the norm. When he pushes Beli-Fachad out into the night (or permits the old man to do so), he once again loses control over the woman's sexuality, and this loss of control is humiliating. His act of dismembering her is an act of reasserting his authority over her body once again (p. 126).

In fact, Bal describes the giving up of Beli-Fachad to her rapists, and the subsequent action of her husband/master as an 'anti-sacrifice'; the woman is 'offered' to the men in order to deflect their violence (p. 123). This sacrifice is antithetical to the sin offerings prescribed in Leviticus. Bal identifies three points of contrast: the burnt offering provided light, but the acts of the men took place at night and ceased in the daylight; the Torah forbade the consumption of the sacrificial victim used in a whole burnt offering, whereas the woman was 'consumed' in an excess of masculine bonding; the sacrifice purified, but the woman was defiled.

There are many elements of Bal's analysis which I find helpful and insightful, and I have drawn upon her ideas throughout this work. However, her overall thesis relies heavily upon the rather idiosyncratic understanding of *pilegesh* as patrilocal wife. In terms of extra-textual support, she cites two main sources. The first is the 1953 lexicon by Koehler and Baumgarter – an excellent resource in its day but one that has been superceded by later editions of Koehler's *HALOT*. In these later editions the idea of patrilocal wife is not offered as a meaning of *pilegesh*.[39] Further, placing too heavy an emphasis on the particular nuance of a word as given in a lexicon is a speculative enterprise, as its placement in the lexicon is a sedimenting action which can conceal the strength or weakness of the underlying scholarship. Dictionary definitions are compiled from the best scholarship of the day, but their definitions do not become 'textus receptus,' though unwary scholars can treat them as such.

The second extra-textual source that Bal uses is a pair of papers by Julian Morgenstern in 1929 and 1931.[40] Morgenstern cites multiple examples from the Hebrew Bible of wives remaining with their fathers or at least considering the possibility that they might do so. Thus: Rebecca is consulted about whether she is willing to leave her father's household to marry Isaac (Genesis 24). Rachel and Leah continue to reside with their father for years after their marriage, and their ultimate departure presents significant difficulties (Genesis 31). Moses lives in his father–in–law's household for years and his wife does not come to Egypt with him in the first instance (Exodus 2:21–22; 4:18; 18:2). Samson's wife remains with her father–in–law and he feels at liberty to redesignate her to a new husband (Judges 14:19–15:2). Gideon appears to have a *beena* wife (Judges 8:31).

The proposal made by Morgenstern and picked up here by Bal does not appear to have gained favour in the scholarly community.[41] Morgenstern's work is now somewhat dated, and his argument is regarded as weak. Most, if not all, of the examples he provides seem to relate to the bridegroom being driven from his home unexpectedly and therefore settling with his wife's family of necessity.[42] Tammi Schneider (Berit Olam commentary), Barry

Webb (NICOT commentary), and Daniel Block (New American Commentary: Judges and Ruth) are all aware of the work of Bal but do not entertain her patrilocal hypothesis. Pamela Reis actively dismisses it as poorly evidenced.[43] Chaim Rabin's careful examination of the etymology and meaning of *pilegesh* makes no reference to *beena* or patrilocal wives.[44]

Overall, it is possible that there are traces of *beena* marriage here but whether we can be confident enough of this to construct an entire thesis of dissymmetry, and whether the prolonged stay of the Levite at his father-in-law's house really reflects a power struggle for the woman (upon which rests the 'horrible' reading of the events of the night), seem to me to be moot. It is in fact hard to imagine that anything could make these events more horrible. Whatever the underlying system of oppression, in the end the woman is violated, abused, and murdered.

Cheryl Exum: raped by the pen

In a magisterial essay, 'Raped by the Pen,' in her book *Fragmented Women*, Cheryl Exum builds a careful, almost forensic case against the writer of Judges, accusing him of raping Beli-Fachad with his pen as surely as her textual attackers did with their bodies.[45] By textual rape, Exum is referring to a way of writing that subjects the woman to the male gaze; that is, that promotes objectification and violence. She juxtaposes the account of Beli-Fachad with that of Bathsheba, suggesting that the narrator deprived both women of their voice and portrayed their characters in an ambiguous light, both of these actions leaving the women open to assault by characters in the story and by later commentators upon the story.

There are six principal elements to Exum's charge against the writer of Judges.

1   The device of leaving Beli-Fachad anonymous is a dehumanising move that has stripped her of her personality.

2   Beli-Fachad's character is smeared by the correspondence of her leaving her father with the word זנה, which, as we have seen previously, represents some sort of sexual impropriety. This character assassination has been aided by translators who have

rendered *pilegesh* as 'concubine' rather than the much more respectable 'secondary wife.'

3   The narrator delivers Beli-Fachad's abuse and dismemberment as a narrative punishment for her expression of sexual autonomy. (Note that the virgin was spared.) 'If one man cannot possess her, then many will.'[46]

4   The Levite's unreliable account of the events is rewarded by the successful muster of the tribes.

5   The woman is portrayed as a chaotic force that precipitates civil war.

6   Our gaze is directed voyeuristically to the dead woman on the doorstep, though the pace of narration of the events of the treatment of her body are an avoidance technique for our comfort, which allows us to view the dismemberment with detachment.

Exum concludes that although the narrator is not consciously misogynistic, his 'underlying male fear of female sexuality'[47] motivates the subtext of this tale. Further, the narrator assumes that the *pilegesh* is responsible for her own fate.

> By insinuating that women [. . .] by the way they behave, are responsible for male sexual behaviour, our [text relies] on a fundamental patriarchal strategy for exercising social control over women.[48]

In the end, Exum concedes that 'literary rape is difficult to prove'[49] and requires taking the woman's word for it. By attempting to give voice to the *pilegesh*, Exum is aiming to allow her to assert her objectification by the text and make the accusation herself.

Exum's argument is forceful and attractive. It effectively uncovers the ways that the text has made itself prone to misrepresenting Beli-Fachad's character, conduct, and value. And Exum does not seek to impugn the intentions of the narrator, but rather the patriarchal constraints within which he writes and to which he is blind.

> I do not suggest that the biblical narrators set out to violate the female characters they created, and, indeed, there may be many

critics who will come to their defense. In calling these stories literary rape, the woman critic attempts to give voice to biblical women whose experience has been suppressed and distorted by androcentric texts.[50]

However, there may be other ways to give voice to Beli-Fachad, or rather to uncover her voice. So, as a complement to the approaches offered by Bal and Exum, we will now explore the possibilities of reading reparatively.

Notes

1 Scholz, *Sacred Witness*, 210.
2 Bal, *Death and Dissymmetry*, 28.
3 Yairah Amit, *The Book of Judges: The Art of Editing*, trans. Jonathan Chipman (Leiden: Brill, 1999), 341.
4 J. Alberto Soggin, *Judges, a Commentary*, trans. John Bowden (London: SCM Press, 1981), 261; C. F. Burney, *The Book of Judges with Introduction and Notes* (New York: KTAV Publishing House, 1918 (1970 edition.)).
5 Tammi Schneider, *Judges: Berit Olam Commentary* (Collegeville: Liturgical Press, 2000), 245–69; Barry G. Webb, *The Book of Judges, An Integrated Reading: JSOT Suppl. 46* (Sheffield: Sheffield Academic Press, 1987). For a detailed discussion of the issues and survey of scholarly opinion on this matter, see Trent C. Butler, *Word Biblical Commentary, Volume 8: Judges* (Nashville: Word, 2009), xliii–lxiv.
6 Bal, *Death and Dissymmetry*, 13.
7 Soggin, *Judges*, 261.
8 Denis the Carthusian, *Enarrationes in Judicum*. Quoted in Joy A. Schroeder, *Dinah's Lament: The Biblical Legacy of Sexual Violence in Christian Interpretation* (Minneapolis: Fortress Press, 2007), 127 (emphasis added).
9 Matthew Henry, *Matthew Henry's Commentary on the Whole Bible: Complete and Unabridged in One Volume* (Peabody: Hendrickson, 1994), 367 (emphasis added).
10 George F. Moore, *A Critical and Exegetical Commentary on Judges* (Edinburgh: T&T Clark, 1895), 424 (italics original).
11 This use of language will be critiqued later on.
12 Simon J. Robinson, *Opening Up Judges* (Leominster: Day One Publications, 2006), 113.
13 Block, *Judges, Ruth*, 543.
14 Michael Wilcock, *The Message of Judges: Grace Abounding. The Bible Speaks Today* (Nottingham: Inter-Varsity Press, 1992), 169.
15 Quotation is from *New King James Study Bible* (Grand Rapids: Zondervan, 2018 (electronic edition), note on Judges 19:4; See, likewise, Ralferd C. Freytag, "The Hebrew Prophets and Sodom and Gomorrah," *Consensus* 32, no. 2 (2008).

16 Soggin, *Judges*, 282.

17 Robert G. Boling, *Judges: Introduction, Translation, and Commentary*, Anchor Bible Commentary, Vol. 6A (New Haven: Yale University Press, 2008), 277–79.

18 Robert A. Watson, *The Book of Judges and Ruth* (Hartford: S. S. Scranton, 1903), 829–33.

19 Adam Clarke, *Judges* (Albany: Ages Software, 1999 (electronic edition)), note on Judges 19:26.

20 Where it has an indirect object, זנה generally takes בְּ, אֶל, or אַחֲרֵי but this is to indicate the individual with whom the person was unfaithful (or, where the word is used of metaphorical, cultic, infidelity, the object of idolatry). Thus, for example, Ezekiel 16:17 וַתִּזְנִי־בָם (and with them you played the whore); Numbers 25:1 וַיָּחֶל הָעָם לִזְנוֹת אֶל־בְּנוֹת מוֹאָב (the people began to whore with the daughters of Moab); Exodus 34:15 וְזָנוּ אַחֲרֵי אֱלֹהֵיהֶם (they whored after their gods). The direct object of the sexual transgression (the 'wronged party,' i.e. the husband or father) is indicated with the direct object marker אֶת־. Thus Leviticus 21:9 כִּי תֵחֵל לִזְנוֹת אֶת־אָבִיהָ (if she defiles herself by playing the whore against her father).

21 For a comprehensive discussion, see Isabelle Hamley, "What's Wrong with 'Playing the Harlot'? The Meaning of זנה in Judges 19:2," *Tyndale Bulletin* 66, no. 1 (2015): 41–62; Butler, *Judges,* 419.

22 Schroeder, *Dinah's Lament*, 101–52.

23 In modern English: 'lewd deed [. . .] on the morrow, when she saw herself so shamed and defiled, she died of sorrow.'

24 In more modern English: 'And therefore every woman ought to restrain wrath and to please and suffer her husband, if he be wroth, with fair language, and not to go away from him, as that woman did, of which came much sorrow, as the death of herself and of so great number of people.' Geoffroy de la Tour Landry, *The Book of the Knight of La Tour-Landry, Compiled for the Instruction of His Daughters*, trans. Thomas Wright (London: Kegan Paul, Trench, Trubner & Co, 1906), Chapter LXII, 94.

25 Johannes Brentz, Operum Reverendi et Clarissimi Theologogi, translated and quoted in Schroeder, *Dinah's Lament*, 139.

26 Martin Bucer, In Librum Iudicum Enarrationes, translated and quoted in Schroeder, *Dinah's Lament,* 141.

27 Keith L. Brooks, *Summarized Bible: Complete Summary of the Old Testament* (Los Angeles: Bible Institute of Los Angeles, 2009), 55.

28 Butler, *Judges*, 421.

29 Genesis 25:1.

30 1 Chronicles 1:32.

31 A similar conclusion is drawn in V. H. Matthews and D. C. Benjamin, *Social World of Ancient Israel 1260–587* (Peabody: Hendrickson, 1993), 14.

32 Bal, *Death and Dissymmetry*, 80–86.

33 The term is first used in Sara Ahmed, *The Promise of Happiness* (Durham: Duke University Press, 2010).

34 The term 'hermeneutics of suspicion' is an interpretive approach which reads a text against the grain with the intention of uncovering the ideologies it contains.

35 Bal, *Death and Dissymmetry*.

36 Bal likens her work to that of a psychoanalyst who seeks to uncover repressed memory. This model is very similar to the one described as 'paranoid' by Eve Sedgwick, as we shall see in Chapter 3.

37 This style of marriage is described in Matthews and Benjamin, *Social World of Ancient Israel 1260–587*, 14. Confusingly, however, they refer to this as 'matrilocal,' and the form of marriage which Bal calls 'virilocal' Matthews and Benjamin describe as 'patrilocal.'

38 This concept of 'rapeability' is not antithetical to the idea of 'unrapeability' used in Chapter 5. Rapeability here means useable for men by sexual purposes. Unrapeability, as it is used later, refers to the idea that such use does not constitute the crime of rape.

39 L. Koehler, W. Baumgartner, M. E. J. Richardson, and J. J. Stamm, *The Hebrew and Aramaic Lexicon of the Old Testament* (Leiden: E. J. Brill, 1994–2000), 929.

40 Julian Morgenstern, "Beena Marriage (Matriarchat) in Ancient Israel and Its Historical Implications," *Zeitschrift für die Alttestamentliche Wissenschaft* 47, no. 1 (1929): 91–110; Julian Morgenstern, "Additional Notes on Beena Marriage (Matriarchat) in Ancient Israel," *Zeitschrift für die alttestamentliche Wissenschaft* 49, no. 1 (1931): 46–58.

41 Tammi Schneider (*Berit Olam commentary*), Barry Webb (*NICOT commentary*), and Daniel Block (*New American Commentary: Judges and Ruth*) are all aware of the work of Bal but do not entertain her patrilocal hypothesis.

42 Louis M. Epstein, "The Hebrew Family: A Study in Historical Sociology by Earle Bennett Cross (Review)," *The Jewish Quarterly Review* 20, no. 4 (1930): 367–71.

43 Pamela T. Reis, "The Levite's Concubine: New Light on a Dark Story," *Scandinavian Journal of the Old Testament* 20, no. 1 (2006): 130–31.

44 Chaim Rabin, "The Origin of the Hebrew Word Pileges," *Journal of Jewish Studies* 25, no. 3 (1974): 353–64.

45 Exum, *Fragmented Women*, 170–201.

46 Exum, *Fragmented Women*, 181.

47 Exum, *Fragmented Women*, 181.

48 Exum, *Fragmented Women*, 189.

49 Exum, *Fragmented Women*, 200.

50 Exum, *Fragmented Women*, 201.

3 Opening up redemptive possibilities

Eve Kosofsky Sedgwick, who died prematurely in 2009, was an American critical theorist who worked particularly in the areas of gender studies and queer theory. In 1997, Sedgwick published an influential introduction to an edited volume on queer affect theory, *Novel Gazing: Queer Readings in Fiction*. This was an expansion of an earlier, shorter essay and was itself slightly reworked in 2003. In these papers she set out the technique she terms 'reparative reading.' In this chapter, we will examine what Sedgwick means by this and then consider the partially reparative approach offered by Phyllis Trible in her highly acclaimed and astonishing work, *Texts of Terror*.

Eve Sedgwick: good surprises

In all three versions of her paper, Sedgwick borrowed language from psychoanalyst Melanie Klein to advocate a move away from so-called paranoid interpretive approaches. Paranoid readings anticipate problems in the text so that there may be no unpleasant surprises. This effectively is another term for readings derived from a suspicious hermeneutic. As Sedgwick describes them, paranoid readings tend to fulfil the negative expectation of the reader; if the reader is looking for trouble, she is likely to find it. A paranoid reading is tautological, or circular: the stronger the resistance that the text presents, the more entrenched becomes the reader's paranoia.

A paranoid position places stress on the discovery, or exposure, of the pathologies of the text. Sedgwick questions the value of such an emphasis, for it depends upon the reading taking place within a cultural context where violence is deprecated and hence disguised. However, where violence is public and serves a communicative purpose, the paranoid position is less helpful, and may indeed increase pain. Thus Sedgwick writes of

> [Paranoia's] cruel and contemptuous assumption that the one thing lacking for global revolution, explosion of gender roles, or whatever, is people's (that is, *other* people's) having the painful effects of their oppression, poverty, or deludedness sufficiently exacerbated to make the pain conscious (as if otherwise it wouldn't have been) and intolerable (as if intolerable situations were famous for generating excellent solutions).[1]

The alternative that Sedgwick offers is reparative reading, which, in psychoanalytic terms, seeks pleasure rather than forestalling pain. Reparative readings are less aggressive than paranoid ones, and less driven by pre-existing theses. The possibility remains open of good surprises; of discovering a richness of textual opportunity rather than a monopolising closure.

A reparative reading does not require the disavowal of one's pre-commitment to a particular ideological position. Rather, it requires an openness to the possibilities of how that ideology might intersect with the text and a willingness to offer a thick interpretation of it. And it opens up the possibility of moving forward beyond mere critique.

> For someone to have an unmystified, angry view of large and genuinely systemic oppressions does not *intrinsically* or *necessarily* enjoin on that person any specific train of epistemological or narrative consequences.[2]

Reparative readings are not easy to do and may not always be desirable. Jennifer Knust performed a test case for reparative reading upon the story of the Curse of Canaan in Genesis 9. This text has had a florid and problematic political afterlife, having been used to bolster arguments for black slavery and the abrogation of black civil rights. However, even after stripping away the accretions of generations of ideological interpretation, enough traces of racism were present in the original text that Knust concluded she could not bring herself to attempt to like it. In the end, she *wanted* to be paranoid about it.

> The concentrated efforts of biblical scholars to identify and expunge false racism from the comparatively mild xenophobia of the biblical text does not so much undermine that racism as create a set of readers who can love the Bible despite whatever kernel of hate might be buried there.[3]
>
> I refuse to convene, assemble or meet up with anyone who likes Genesis 9, and invite you to join me in my paranoid dissatisfaction.[4]

In a methodological evaluation of Sedgwick's article, Knust points out the ironical paranoia of her (Sedgwick's) position, which reads the paranoid interpretations with mistrust. This extends even as far as the mimesis within Sedgwick's essay subtitle, 'You're So Paranoid, You Probably Think This Introduction Is About You':

> Anticipating paranoia's disastrous effect, she turns it back on 'you,' a classically paranoid move, if ever there was one.[5]

Knust suggests that the reparative approach always needs to be balanced with the paranoid, because they are constitutive and corollaries of one another. She rightly doubts that a reparative reading can ever be conducted wholly in the absence of the paranoid; rather, the two are complementary.[6]

As a complement, then, to the paranoid – or at least suspicious – interpretations of Exum and Bal, I will here explore the possibilities of a reparative approach to the text.

Phyllis Trible: repent, repent

Close to a reparative reading, perhaps, is the approach of Phyllis Trible in her deservedly influential book *Texts of Terror*, which examines four biblical texts of male-on-female violence.[7] Trible reads closely, with awareness of the literary aspects of the narrative and with close attention to the female characters in the texts. I consider her approach to be partially reparative because it is constructive: she views her work as in some way establishing a textual memoriam to the assaulted women of the stories. She uses the biblical story of Jacob at the ford of Jabbok to describe her conviction that there is blessing to be wrested from the encounter.

> We struggle mightily, only to be wounded. But yet we hold on, seeking a blessing: the healing of wounds and the restoration of health.[8]

Trible examines the story of Beli-Fachad in close detail, particularly noting her exclusion from the discourse, from the decision making, from the benefits of hospitality, and from the attention of the narrator. She then considers five levels of response to the story: the response of tribal Israel (multiplication of violence); the evaluation of the editor of the book of Judges (he uses it to promote the monarchy); the response by the shapers of the canon (the juxtaposition with the story of Hannah in the Hebrew Bible and with Ruth in the Greek Bible, which both speak 'healing words'); the response of the prophets (a meagre and elliptical critique by Hosea); and from the rest of scripture (silence, which she considers to be complicity). Finally, she turns to the response of the reader, and urges that this might be redemptive. 'Repent! Repent! [. . .] We must take counsel to say, "Never again"' (p. 87).

Notwithstanding this reclamation of good that Trible urges, she cannot wholly escape the charge of being a suspicious reader – nor, I think, would she want to. In particular, she is quick to attribute to the writer of the text the motives and ideology of the characters within the text. This is most clear when we compare her observations on this story with her comments about Tamar, raped by her half-brother. Trible, like Exum, considers that Beli-Fachad is denied subjectivity because she is silenced by the narrator. But Tamar, who does speak in resistance of her treatment, is praised by Trible for her wisdom, while the narrator, who has given her this voice, receives no commendation. This is a suspicious conclusion and, I think, an unfair one. Why would the narrator of Samuel not be praised for giving voice to the female victim, when the narrator of Judges receives criticism for failing to do so?

This blurring of the levels at which criticism is directed is not uncommon. But a distinction should be drawn between the ideology of the characters or of the society they inhabit and the ideology of the narrator (of the text itself); and between these and the ideologies of the text's interpreters. Certainly, the ideologies may align. But equally they may not. It is entirely possible to tell a story of misogynistic abuse without being misogynistic.[9] It is also possible to tell a story of misogynistic abuse without intending to evoke misogyny in the reader. As Erik Eynikel puts it,

> [Trible] does not understand the quasi-objective narration and the precise description of horrors is [...] a much more effective critique of violence than snorting out moral indignation, nor that the narrator is morally in order by the very creation and handing down of this story.[10]

Readings such as Trible's have failed to identify the critical distance sometimes taken by the text towards the society it is narrating, notwithstanding the inescapable fact that it is also shaped by such unspoken androcentrism. Indeed, the ability of the text to escape, partially, from that androcentrism, and take a sternly censorious glance at the events it is describing, should heighten our appreciation for its critical stance.

A reparative reader, as conceived by Sedgwick, can deplore an oppressive ideology as wholly as a paranoid reader. Trible's account of the *pilegesh* begins to move in a partly reparative direction. In the following two chapters we will seek to develop a reparative reading more fully.

Notes

1 Eve Kosovsky Sedgwick, "Paranoid Reading and Reparative Reading: Or, You're so Paranoid, You Probably Think This Introduction Is About You," in *Novel Gazing: Queer Readings in Fiction,* ed. Eve Kosovsky Sedgwick (Durham: Duke University Press, 1997), 20.
2 Sedgwick, "Paranoid Reading," 3.
3 Jennifer Knust, "Who's Afraid of Canaan's Curse? Genesis 9:18–29 and the Challenge of Reparative Reading," *Biblical Interpretation* 22 (2014): 408.
4 Knust, "Who's Afraid," 410.

5 Knust, "Who's Afraid," 388–413.

6 See Robyn Wiegman, "The Times We're in: Queer Feminist Criticism and the Reparative 'Turn'," *Feminist Theory* 15, no. 1 (2014): 4–25.

7 Phyllis Trible, *Texts of Terror: Literary-feminist Readings of Biblical Narratives* (London: SCM Press, 1984).

8 Trible, *Texts of Terror*, 4–5.

9 This is similar to the point made by Robert Alter, who encourages the reader to note the difference between the narrator's voice and the speech of the characters within the narrative. Robert Alter, *The Art of Biblical Narrative* (London: George Allen & Unwin, 1981), 77.

10 Erik Eynikel, "Judges 19–21, an 'Appendix': Rape, Murder, War and Abduction," *Communio Viatorum* 47 (2005): 103.

4 Beli-Fachad as subject and object

In her book *Claiming her Dignity: Female Resistance in the Old Testament*, Juliana Claassens explores ways in which the women of the Hebrew Bible who are subjected to the dehumanising effects of war, rape, heterarchy, and precarity express themselves in resistance.[1] She relates this to the 'hidden transcripts' discussed by James Scott, whereby the oppressed find creative ways to express their subversive discourse of resistance in places where it is unobserved by the power brokers.[2]

However, Claassens focusses her attention mainly on the actions of the women *within* the events of the discourse. Within the chapter on rape, for example, she examines Tamar's story (2 Samuel 13) and the apocryphal story of Susanna (found in Daniel 13). Claassens argues that defiance is expressed by verbal resistance, embodied mourning, determined survival with a refusal to be defined by a single moment of victimhood, and defence by a noble man. These acts of defiance cause the reader to imagine a world where no woman is raped.[3]

Unfortunately for Beli-Fachad, few of these acts of resistance can be said to apply to her. She is not shown to resist her attackers, she does not survive to testify by her defiant presence, and she is not defended by any of the men in her life. She does, briefly, embody mourning but this is extremely transitory and unwitnessed by the characters in the narrative (assuming that she is dead by the time the Levite comes out of the house in the morning).

Moving from the level of the text to the level of the narrator, Cheryl Exum argues that Beli-Fachad continues to be violated beyond the events of the narrative, by the author himself.[4] As we have seen, she builds this argument with attention to the use of anonymity, character assassination, punishment motif, and pornographic objectification, in addition to the 'rewarding' of the dishonest Levite and the representation of the woman as a chaotic, war-inducing force. In particular, Exum says, 'the denial of subjectivity is an important factor in rape.'[5] And Beli-Fachad is most certainly acted upon. Indeed, as Foucault might suggest, in her rape and dismemberment her body becomes the page on which others inscribe their discourse.[6] And as one who is defined in terms of her relationship to her man, however we construe that relationship, she has been *constructed* by the power relations in which she is held.[7] As Judith Butler describes it,

> The cultural construction of the body is effected through the figuration of 'history' as a writing instrument that produces cultural significations — language — through the disfiguration and distortion of the body, where the body is figured as a ready surface or blank page available for inscription, awaiting the 'imprint' of history itself.[8]

By these accounts then, Beli-Fachad's failure to exercise any resistive practice, and her denial of subjectivity by the narrator, mean that she is simply a passive victim whose story may represent little reparative potential.

But is Beli-Fachad as objectified as this implies? In the remainder of this chapter, we will consider the interplay of objectification and subjectivity which is present throughout this account. We will consider the role of anonymity and Beli-Fachad's surprising moral and marital agency. In the chapter that follows we will consider her subjectivity in discourse. I will aim to argue that, far from being wholly objectified by characters and narrator, she exercises remarkable subjectivity, and the designation of textual rape is not an inevitable conclusion from the evidence.

Anonymity

It is often argued that Beli-Fachad's anonymity is evidence of her lack of subjectivity. For example, Cheryl Exum argues that this namelessness encourages readers to overlook her.[9] Trible notes that the *pilegesh* is not the only anonymous character in the narrative but nonetheless considers that her namelessness and speechlessness show the storyteller's indifference to her.[10] With reference to the daughter of Jephthah, another anonymous female figure in Judges, Mieke Bal speaks of the need to name her because failure to do so would endorse the inherent ideology of the text.[11]

But anonymity can serve its own rhetorical purpose. Don Hudson offers five reasons why anonymous figures biblical narrative are sometimes anonymous: because they are minor characters, to focus or quicken the plot, to focus on and highlight other characters, to 'universalise' the characters and events of the narrative, and to parallel the loss of identity and personhood that the character is experiencing in the narrative.[12] He suggests that the last two of these apply to Beli-Fachad: her anonymity universalises the story, to show how it might have applied to anyone in the day, and it provides a literary parallel to the chaos and dehumanisation that she is experiencing.

> By viewing the anonymity of the concubine the reader gets the impression that 'every' concubine from Dan to Beersheba could be raped, murdered and dismembered.[13]

In her study of anonymity in biblical narrative, Adele Reinhartz expresses both positive and negative points of view:

> The anonymity of this woman can be seen as symbolic of her silence, the progressive passivity attributed to her, and the tragic fate with which the story culminates. These features combine to efface her identity and her very existence.[14]
>
> The absence of all personal names lends this section a legendary, paradigmatic quality. This quality endows the characters and the events in which they participate with a significance which is unrelated to their individuality. [. . .] The general

anonymity suggests that the individual identities of these figures are not as important as the fact that the events in which
they participate occurred in a kingless nation.[15]

However, to say anonymity is a device to highlight a paradigm is
one thing; to claim it is thereby obliterative is surely to overstate
the case. If anonymity is serving to generalise the story, to cast
upon the woman an exemplary role, then this would seem to
accentuate rather than obliterate her importance within the narrative. Indeed, it might be argued that the very insinuation of her
unimportance through the device of anonymity simultaneously
asserts her importance in a rather neat demonstration of Derrid-
ean undecidability.[16]

If the woman's anonymity is a coded message that women
were gang-raped to death on a regular basis in those days, then
the anonymity of her husband serves a reciprocal purpose in
relation to his exemplary role. Here Reinhartz argues that the
narrator is critical in its appraisal of him: 'The anonymity of this
Levite man [. . .] focusses attention on the dissonance between
his double designations, as man and as Levite, and his behaviour, which perverts the typified role associates with these designations.'[17] And Pamela Reis concludes that 'the technique of
namelessness illustrates the disintegration and dehumanization
of society.'[18]

So anonymity may not, inherently, be objectifying. What of Beli-
Fachad's actions within the story? For she is not solely the subject
of passive verbs.

Moral and marital agency

At the beginning of Judges 19, Beli-Fachad leaves her husband
and returns to the house of her father. We will shortly discuss the
possible reasons for this abandonment, but first let us note how
extraordinary it is. In Hebrew custom and law, there is provision
for a man to put his wife aside, but not the reverse. For example, Deuteronomy 22:13–21 describes the procedure for treating
a woman who is not found to be a virgin on her wedding night.
Deuteronomy 24:1–4 provides for a man to divorce his wife, but

not the other way around. So, here, Beli-Fachad is operating with remarkable autonomy and agency.[19] And there is a textual indicator to support this reading of feminine agency.

> Her husband arose and went after her, to speak to her heart.
>
> (19:3)

The phrase 'her husband' is unexpected. Throughout the remainder of the narrative, she is repeatedly referred to as 'his *pilegesh*' (vv.2, 9, 10, 24, 25, 27, 29), but here, he is אִישָׁהּ 'her husband/man.'[20] In fact, this female possessive pronoun on the noun is only found within seven other biblical narratives.[21] They are as follows:

- Eve giving the fruit to her husband (Genesis 3:6)
- Sarah giving Hagar to her husband (Genesis 16:3)
- The annunciation scene in which Samson's mother receives a visit from an angel and calls her husband (Judges 13:9,10)
- Elkanah is described as Hannah's husband (1 Samuel 1:8,22; 2:19)
- Bathsheba mourns over Uriah her husband (2 Samuel 11:26)
- The Shunammite is described as the husband of a woman who provides hospitality to Elisha (2 Kings 4:9,22)
- Naomi attempts to send Ruth and Orpah back to remarry and each live in the house of her (new) husband; Boaz is described as a relative of Naomi's husband (Ruth 1:9, 2:1)

It is striking that these are all scenes of strong female agency. Eve, Sarah, Hannah, the Shunammite's wife, Naomi, and Ruth are all particularly proactive women within their narratives. Bathsheba is a very significant figure, although the extent of her proactivity in the seduction narrative is debated. Samson's mother is a minor character, but, unusually, it is she rather than her husband whom that the angel visits and the one to whose knowledge her husband is instructed to defer (Judges 13:13). They are also (with the exception of the Shunammite woman) women whose stories are highly important in the developing story of Israel; they represent and are the means of great turning points in history.

There is further support for this in 20:4 where the Levite is referred to as אִישׁ הָאִשָּׁה (husband of the woman/wife), a phrase which appears to be unattested anywhere else in the Hebrew Bible. In fact, the sentence carries redundancy in order to make the point. A very literal translation would read:

The man, the Levite, husband of the murdered woman.

It would not be unusual for the word 'man' to be qualified with 'the Levite' or some other description, but here the narrator heaps qualifiers on top of one another, making the designation quite emphatic.

There appear to be textual clues, then, that Beli-Fachad is operating with strong agency. However, this emphasis, and hence the woman's agency, has been obliterated by certain translators; the Good News Translation has 'the Levite whose concubine had been murdered,' and the New English Bible renders it 'the Levite, to whom the woman belonged.' They have overlooked the force of 'the husband of the woman' and inverted the relationship of belonging.

But what is the cause of her abandonment of her husband/master? As we saw earlier, the reason is unclear. She may have been returning home to resume a patrilocal pattern of marriage. She may have been angry with him (why?), she may have been unfaithful to him (if so, why did her father take her in?), or he may possibly have been pimping her out.[22]

As we have seen, the suspicion of sexual impropriety and the woman's abandonment of her husband/master have led many commentators to view the events that unfold as narrative punishment for her. Some endorse this, as we saw in the review of traditional commentary upon the text. Others, such as Cheryl Exum, deprecate it. In Exum's view, the narrator delivers Beli-Fachad up to abuse and dismemberment as a narrative punishment for her expression of sexual autonomy – note that the virgin daughter was spared. 'If one man cannot possess her, then many will.'[23] In similar vein, Fewell and Gunn describe how the Levite might have thrown his woman to the mob as a punishment.

It is not difficult to reconstruct his rationale. If she had not left him, if she had not refused to return on her own so that he was forced to fetch her, and if her father had not detained him, they would not be in this predicament. This is clearly her fault. She must pay the price.[24]

Perhaps as a result, there has been a scramble of commentators in recent years seeking to exonerate Beli-Fachad of sexual impropriety and restore her as the innocent victim.[25] (It has, however, been pointed out that exonerating the *pilegesh* also helps to exonerate the Levite of rather pathetically running after an unfaithful wife.)[26]

So was Beli-Fachad unfaithful, or was she not?[27] Isabelle Hamley points out the false (and dangerous) dichotomy that is set up by the underlying assumption that the collocation of the *pilegesh*'s unfaithfulness and her fate implies causation:

> Linking unfaithfulness and rape causally creates a dilemma: do we condemn the text as one that is utterly insensitive and callous, oppressive to women, and therefore either discard it or amend it, or do we condemn the concubine as guilty and therefore deserving her fate – thereby risking legitimising monstrous behaviour? The dilemma is unnecessary.[28]

As an intriguing third possibility, she offers the possibility that the Masoretic Text remains deliberately ambiguous about the cause of the woman's relocation, and whether she had committed some sort of sexual infidelity or not. In so doing, the *pilegesh*'s moral subjectivity is asserted. Beli-Fachad is not a one-dimensional literary device, but a complex, ambiguous individual.

> To say that no character is guiltless is not to say that they are all morally equal. Furthermore, the idea of a 'guiltless victim' is interesting: linking guilt and victimhood assumes a link between the concubine's behaviour and her eventual fate in Gibeah, as if a 'real victim' must be 'guiltless.'[29]

In other words, a fierce assertion that she is not sexually unfaithful continues to promulgate the paradigm of wicked women receiving due punishment. But in contrast, allowing the moral ambiguity freedom to express itself forces us to reappraise that logic.

In addition, the question of whether she is offended or offender also credits her with moral agency.

> The MT as opposed to the LXX positions her as a *moral* subject in a tale concerned with the breakdown of morality. How she is positioned – offending or offended party – defines the Levite's position with respect to her and shapes an evaluation of his conduct, and others' reaction to her.[30]

As Tammi Schneider says, 'Most scholars simply cannot believe that an Israelite woman would do things that they do not expect her to do.'[31]

Another twist lies in wait. The Masoretes marked verse 3 with a *ketiv-qere*. This means that they made a marginal note suggesting that the text as written (*ketiv*) is corrupt and should be read (*qere*) differently. The *ketiv* says the Levite went after Beli-Fachad 'to speak to her heart to bring *him* back' לַהֲשִׁיבוֹ. However, the marginal note suggests that this should be read 'to bring *her* back' לַהֲשִׁיבָהּ. Most English translations accept the *qere* without even a footnote.[32] But this interpretive decision has stripped Beli-Fachad of her agency which is expressed in the consonantal Hebrew text. He is, it implies, begging that she will take him back.

Mieke Bal urges us to understood how narratives like this one function within the dynamics of an ideology. Although she considers that the women she is studying have no subjectivity at the level of discourse (they do not speak) nor at the level of focalization (their perspective is not recorded),

> [T]here is, however, a third level on which subject-positions are distributed in narrative: the level of the fabula, of what happens, of the events. [. . .] Within the fabula as a series of events [. . .] the event of which they are the objects does have consequences. [. . .] [T]heir relevance as elements in the story has to be assessed.[33]

So the woman can have a significant role within the plot, whereby she moves the plot on and uncovers the unreliability of men and the faithfulness of the nation. In other words, Beli-Fachad has a voice. We will consider this in the next chapter.

Notes

1 Juliana Claassens, *Claiming Her Dignity: Female Resistance in the Old Testament* (Collegeville: Liturgical Press, 2016).

2 James Scott, *Domination and the Arts of Resistance: Hidden Transcripts* (New Haven: Yale University Press, 1990).

3 Claassens, *Claiming*, 34–66.

4 A similar argument is made in Caroline Blyth, "Terrible Silence, Eternal Silence: A Feminist Re-reading of Dinah's Voicelessness in Genesis 34," *Biblical Interpretation* 17, no. 5 (2009): 491–92.

5 Exum, *Fragmented Women,* 173.

6 Michel Foucault, *The History of Sexuality, Volume 1* (New York: Vintage, 1980), 148.

7 Michel Foucault, *Power/Knowledge: Selected Interviews and Other Writings, 1972–1977,* ed. and trans. C. Gordon (New York: Pantheon Books, 1980), 186. Foucault's view of rape is helpfully critiqued in Ann Cahill, "Foucault, Rape, and the Construction of the Feminine Body," *Hypatia* 15, no. 1 (2000): 43–63.

8 Judith Butler, "Foucault and the Paradox of Bodily Inscriptions," *The Journal of Philosophy* 86, no. 11 (1989): 603.

9 Exum, *Fragmented Women,* 176.

10 Trible, *Texts of Terror*, 64–91.

11 Bal, *Death and Dissymmetry*, 43.

12 Don Michael Hudson, "Living in a Land of Epithets: Anonymity in Judges 19–21," *Journal for the Study of the Old Testament* 19, no. 62 (1994): 59.

13 Hudson, "Land of Epithets," 49–60. A similar point is offered by Katherine Southwood, *Marriage by Capture in the Book of Judges: An Anthropological Approach* (Cambridge: Cambridge University Press, 2017), 14.

14 Adele Reinhartz, *"Why Ask My Name?" Anonymity and Identity in Biblical Narrative,* trans. Jonathan Chipman (Oxford: Oxford University Press, 1998), 125.

15 Reinhartz, *Why Ask My Name?* 125–26.

16 See, for example, Jacques Derrida, *Dissemination,* trans. Barbara Johnson (London: Continuum, 1981).

17 Reinhartz, *Why Ask My Name?* 80.

18 Reis, "The Levite's Concubine," 146.

19 Cf. Karla G. Bohmbach, "Conventions/Contraventions: The Meanings of Public and Private for the Judges 19 Concubine," *Journal for the Study of the Old Testament* 24, no. 83 (1999): 89–90.

20 The Hebrew can be translated either way.

21 This analysis includes אִישָׁהּ (her husband) and לְאִישָׁהּ (to her husband).

22 This possibility is offered in Reis, "The Levite's Concubine," 129.

23 Exum, *Fragmented Women,* 181.

24 Danna Nolan Fewell and David M. Gunn, *Gender, Power, and Promise: The Subject of the Bible's First Story* (Nashville: Abingdon Press, 1993), 134.

25 For example, Robert Boling, J. Alberto Soggin, Pamela Reis and Daniel Block.

26 Hamley, *What's Wrong*, 55.

27 Tammi Schneider points out that the idea of 'infidelity' is at odds with the translation of *pilegesh* as 'concubine.' '[W]hile most would translate the previous verse as, "he took to himself a concubine," meaning that she was never his wife, in this verse they assume she was a legitimate wife. [. . .] If she were officially a wife and committed adultery, according to Deut 22:21 the woman should have been stoned to death. There are no rules in the MT governing what is considered adultery or unlawful procedures for a *pilegesh* because it is not a state that the laws recognize or regulate.' Schneider, *Judges*, 250–51.

28 Hamley, *What's Wrong*, 58.

29 Hamley, *What's Wrong*, 55–56.

30 Hamley, *What's Wrong*, 59. See also Trible, *Texts of Terror*, 66–67.

31 Schneider, *Judges*, 250.

32 Interestingly, the Alexandrinus codex of the LXX has τοῦ διαλλάξαι αὐτὴν ἑαυτῷ καὶ ἀπαγαγεῖν αὐτὴν πάλιν πρὸς αὐτόν, 'to restore her to himself and to lead her back again to him,' which appears, as Trent Butler suggests, to attempt to embrace both the *ketiv* and the *qere*. Butler, *Judges*, 407.

33 Bal, *Death and Dissymmetry*, 33.

5 Beli–Fachad in her own voice

It has been commonly said of Beli-Fachad that she has no speech in the narrative and, therefore, that she is denied agency by the narrator. As we have seen, Cheryl Exum argues that her silencing has contributed to the violation of her character and her textual rape.[1]

But the communication that a text performs can take place at a number of levels. One of the most helpful ways to describe this is using the language of speech act theory. In this literary approach, which is attentive to things that texts do, a communicative act is understood to operate in three linked ways: through its locutionary *content*, its illocutionary *force*, and its perlocutionary *effect*. The classic example offered is the sign that reads 'there is a bull in this field.' The locutionary content is clear enough: here is a field, and it contains a bull. The illocutionary force is warning, if addressed to a prospective rambler; and the perlocutionary effect is fear or caution.[2]

However, a complex text may contain a number of illocutionary acts. Speech act theorists such as Kit Barker and Vern Poythress have referred to the need for 'thick descriptions'[3] of texts: interpretations that consider all the illocutionary acts which it performs.[4] These are found at different levels.[5]

- First there are sentential and subsentential illocutions. These are (respectively) speech acts occurring within a sentence or by means of a whole sentence. For example: *There was a man, a Levite, sojourning in the far hill country of Ephraim.*
- Next there are higher-order illocutions, such as when a narrator uses the speech of a person to subvert their characterisation.

An example of this in our text would be when the Levite says, '*I am journeying to the house of the LORD,*' where no such intention has been related to us previously. The force of this is to cast doubt upon his integrity.

• Then there are whole-text illocutions, which should be regarded as the primary communicative action of the text. One of the whole-text illocutions of our text is the critique of the moral standards of Israel.

This is necessarily an oversimplification, as there may be multiple, intersecting examples of each of these; in particular, the whole-text illocutions might themselves be multiple and at different levels.

We saw previously that Phyllis Trible concludes her analysis of Judges 19 by considering the five levels of response to the story (six, including the reader).[6] This invites us to consider which, if any, of these actors Beli-Fachad might be addressing. What are the levels of discourse of this text, and within which is she operative? Using slightly different categories from Trible, I will focus on four levels: discourse within the events of the night; discourse about the events of the night; discourse about the moral state of Israel; and, finally, the address which the text makes to the modern reader. I will argue that it is within the first of these categories only that Beli-Fachad is silenced. As the circles of address broaden, her voice grows and gains strength.

In contrast to this growing voice of Beli-Fachad, the Levite's voice gradually weakens. Moderately forceful in the immediate events of the night and the discourse about it, his character has little to say about the moral state of Israel and almost nothing to say to the modern reader. We will consider his speech first, and then, in more detail, the communication of Beli-Fachad at the four levels of the narrative.

The failed discourse of the Levite

The Levite speaks four times in our narrative (between 19:1 and 20:7). On each occasion his character is revealed a little more. First, we should notice his lack of speech during the prolonged exchange with Beli-Fachad's father. The father speaks four times:

> Sustain your heart with a little bread, and afterwards you can go. [. . .] Be pleased to stay the night, and may your heart be good. [. . .] Sustain your heart, and wait until the day declines. [. . .] Behold, the day is declining to evening. Stay the night. Behold, the day is waning. Stay the night here. May your heart be good. And you can arise early tomorrow for your journey and you go to your tent.
>
> (19:5,6,8,9)

Each time, until the last, the Levite passively acquiesces, his lack of speech suggesting indolence or lack of resolve. Perhaps he is enjoying his father-in-law's lavish hospitality a bit too much.[7] Certainly, when he does finally exert himself to leave, it is so late on the fifth day that they are only able to travel about six miles before dusk forces them to stop.

It is at this point that he makes his first verbal contribution.

> We will not turn aside to a foreign city, which is not of the sons of Israel. Behold, we will cross to Gibeah. Come, we will approach one of the places, and we will stay overnight in Gibeah or in Ramah.
>
> (19:12–13)

They will not, of course, be safe in Gibeah, and may well have been safer in Jebus. The Levite's first speech is deeply ironical, then, in narrative terms, which the reader sees in retrospect or on rereading. In terms of the portrayal of the Levite's character, these words reveal him as unwise, showing what will prove to be a fatal insouciance about their safety within a city of Israel.

The second speech is to the old man who might offer them hospitality.

> We are crossing from Bethlehem in Judah, to the remote part of the hill country of Ephraim. From there I came to Bethlehem in Judah and I am going to the house of the LORD. And no

man has received me into (his) home. And also, there is straw
and fodder for our donkeys, and also there is bread and wine
for me, and for your slave woman, and for the young man with
your servant. Nothing is lacking of any matter.

(19:18–19)

Here, it is instructive to compare what the Levite tells the old
man with what we have been told in the narrative. The Levite
gives an inaccurate account of the purpose of his journey, making no mention of Beli-Fachad, but implying that he is going to
worship, or serve, at the shrine at Shiloh. The narrator has made
no mention of any such intention. This discrepancy has caused
some commentators to prefer the Septuagintal text (τὸν οἶκόν
μου *my house*) over the Masoretic text (בֵּית יְהֹוָה *the house of the
LORD*).[8]

But this is to miss the point. The ancient writer, redactor, and
Masoretes will not have been less aware of the surprising nature
of these words than modern commentators, and they have allowed
the surprise to remain.[9] Amending the text when something unexpected occurs should be the final resort, not the first. Better to
use the narrative technique pioneered by Meir Sternberg, and pay
attention to the discrepancy between speech and represented world,
considering whether it might be revealing something about the
character of the speaker.[10] It is more likely that the Levite feels
ashamed of the purpose of his journey (it would, after all, amount to
an admission that he had failed to keep good order in his home) and
so he massages the truth to represent himself more favourably to his
host. He certainly goes out of his way to ingratiate himself in the
second half of the speech, emphasising how self-reliant his party is.

Now we encounter another period of disturbing silence. Just as
the Levite quietly acquiesced with his father-in-law's excessive hospitality, so now he quietly acquiesces as the old man remonstrates
with his would-be attackers on his behalf. It is not until the dreadful
events of the night are over that he speaks again, as he prepares to
continue his journey.

Get up. Let's go.

(19:28)

It hardly needs stating that these two brutal words reveal a stagger-
ing depth of indifference and lack of compassion to the woman
whose plight should have evoked the deepest pity even if she had
not been suffering it to ensure his own safety.

Finally, the Levite addresses the nation, which he has mustered by
sending out the dismembered remains of the woman.

> To Gibeah in Benjamin I came, I and my *pilegesh*, to spend
> the night. And the rulers of Gibeah arose against me and
> surrounded the house against me by night. Me, they intended
> to kill! But my *pilegesh* they treated violently and she died. So
> I took my *pilegesh* and cut her up and sent her to every territory
> of the inheritance of Israel. For they have done an infamy and a
> sacrilege in Israel. Behold you sons of Israel, give for yourselves
> counsel and advice here.
>
> (20:4–7)

Once again, it is instructive to compare his account of events
with what the narrator has told us. First, the Levite suggests that
the attack was an organised one involving Gibeah's leading citi-
zens, rather than an unruly rabble.[11] (Compare 20:4 'the rulers
of Gibeah' with 'sons of Belial' in 19:22.) Next, he implies there
was a threat to his own life, though there is no direct evidence
for that in the narrative. In fact, the fronting of the first-person
pronoun, which does not come through clearly in most translations, is narcissistically emphatic. It might be rendered, 'They
intended to kill *me*!', placing the focus upon the threat he felt
rather than the violence Beli-Fachad experienced. Further, he
entirely glosses over his own role in the events of the night,
implying that his *pilegesh* was somehow seized by the mob, rather
than confessing that he was the one that put her out. He also
glosses over the nature of Beli-Fachad's experience: 'they treated
her violently' rather than (v.25) 'they raped her and abused her.'
The dangerous ambiguity about the cause of her death remains,
however: 'and she died.'

This characterisation of the Levite leads Cheryl Exum to call
him self-serving, base, irresolute, callous, and deceitful.[12] Stuart
Lasine considers the 'glaring contradiction[s]' between his words

and the events they purport to describe to be part of a parodic textual critique of the Levite's character.

> While the 'facts' reported by the Levite in Judges 20 are not consistent with Judges 19, the character of the Levite revealed through his speech is totally harmonious with the preceding chapter. He remains totally self-absorbed and indifferent to the women who was murdered because he threw her to the mob to save herself.[13]

Lasine helpfully draws out what many commentators have failed to notice.[14] (The failure to identify the critique of the Levite perhaps supports Mieke Bal's argument for a patriarchal coherence shared by the text and its commentators.[15]) The actions of the Levite are not simply reprehensible in our modern eyes. They are narrated to us in such a way that we have no good reason to doubt the author's own, highly critical, view of them.

The Levite's words are effective: the people prepare for war. For, as Beli-Fachad gradually decreases in power through the narrative, the Levite's power increases.[16] But as his speeches reveal, his character does not match up to his influence. His words are powerful but untrustworthy. He deceives; manipulates; misrepresents; and, with one final 'violent lie,'[17] manipulates the nation into near self-destruction. Does he seek this end at the outset? No, but his utter self-absorption makes him reckless to the consequences of his words and his actions.

We will now, in contrast, consider the powerful and truthful speech of Beli-Fachad.

Beli-Fachad's silencing in the events of the night

As has been described many times, Beli-Fachad does not speak once in the event of Judges 19. She gives no explanation to us of her flight to her father's house. Her response to the arrival of her husband/master is not recorded. Her wishes about staying or leaving her father's house are not consulted. Her opinion on whether to rest at Jebus or Gibeah (or elsewhere) is not obtained. Her fear at the arrival of the mob is not expressed. Her protest at her incipient danger is not heard. Her screams do not reach our notice. Her cry for readmittance to the house is not audible. Her dying gasps do not disturb our peace.

What does silence within a text indicate? Thomas Huckin has identified five possibilities.

> *Speech–act silences* are those that have illocutionary force by virtue of being so interpretable by a reader/listener using [. . .] pragmatic principles; *presuppositional silences* are those that serve communicative efficiency by not stating what the speaker/ writer apparently assumes to be common knowledge; *discreet silences* are those that avoid stating sensitive information; *genre based silences* are those that are governed by genre conventions; and *manipulative silences* are those that deliberately conceal relevant information from the reader/listener.[18]

A paranoid interpretation of the text will assume that the silence of Beli-Fachad is either genre based or manipulative; either the voice of a woman is routinely omitted from the genre, or the narrator has intentionally suppressed it. The 'routine omission' argument does not really hold here, as the broader text of Judges gives voice to women on many occasions, sometimes even prolonged speech (e.g. Judges 5). It could be argued, however, that the female voice is *generally* subordinated to the male voice in this type of literature and that what we are discovering here is another (extreme) example of such subordination. Alternatively, perhaps the woman's voice has been deliberately suppressed within the text. In order for this to be plausible, it would be important to argue that this suppression serves the broader intention of the narrator. Is it perhaps the silence of a woman gagged for pornographic purposes? Is it the silence that overrides her protest because the text is endorsing her treatment?

Cheryl Exum who, as we have seen, makes much of Beli-Fachad's silencing, leans towards the genre explanation.

> By portraying the men of Gibeah as depraved and the Levite as base and insensitive, the narrator of Judges 19 allows us to feel moral outrage at their behaviour – and this is, I think, his goal: to present his audience with a compelling illustration of

the depravity of the times. But his illustration is also typical of the way violence against women is presented, as if gender bias is not an issue.[19]

But Exum seems uncertain whether the narrator is indeed indifferent, or is prurient, suggesting that the *pilegesh*, fallen on the threshold of the house where she took shelter, is 'focalized through the male gaze.'[20] She considers the Levite's callous dismemberment to be pornographic.

> If this scene and the gang rape that precedes it were portrayed in film today, we would label it pornographic. We see the woman fall down at the door after an entire night of sexual abuse. The focus on one part of her body, the accusing hands, is a prelude to the division of the body into parts. [. . .] In pornographic literature and in actual cases, rape and other violent crimes against women are frequently accompanied by bodily mutilation.[21]

However, this is not pornography by any modern definition of the term. In their 1983 Minneapolis Ordinance, Andrea Dworkin and Catherine MacKinnon describe pornography as 'the graphic sexually explicit subordination of women through pictures and/or words.'[22] Although Dworkin and MacKinnon proceed to list one of the variant forms of pornography as 'women [. . .] presented as sexual objects tied up or cut up or mutilated or bruised or physically hurt,' their cardinal feature of *graphic, sexually explicit* subordination appears to me to be absent from this narrative. Indeed, the focus upon Beli-Fachad's hands, emphasised by Exum, could be considered a courteous metonymy for the stricken body. In fact, Exum herself appears to be somewhat ambivalent on the matter, later emphasising the 'fast pace of the consecutive verbs used to describe the mutilation, so that we need not dwell on the explicit details.'[23]

So there is doubt, at least, about the reason for Beli-Fachad's silence in the events of the night. There is room for the possibility that her protest is not heard because it is presupposed (we are told what will surprise us, such as the men's actions, not what we very well know). And there is room for the possibility that her screams are omitted out of discretion.

There is one further possibility: that she *cannot* speak; that her experience has rendered her incapable of speech. Elaine Scarry has described how the nature of pain of this order pushes a person's capacity to speak into a reverse toward the primal utterance of cry and groan:

> Physical pain does not simply resist language but actively destroys it, bringing about an immediate reversion to a state anterior to language, to the sounds and cries a human being makes before language is learned.[24]

This inexpressibility renders the pain of the suffering subject liable to be overlooked and misunderstood, stripped of political agency and desubjectified. Indeed, we have seen just such a decentring of Beli-Fachad's experience in our review of the work of traditional commentators. With reference to modern victims of torture, Scarry points out that the lack of adequate language to describe their physical experience causes systematic misdescriptions of torture, which in turn perpetuate the victimisation. It is important then, that we discover Beli-Fachad's voice is operational at three other levels of discourse.

Beli–Fachad speaks to Israel

We previously considered the unreliable voice of the Levite in his account to Israel of the events of the night. By contrast, the body of Beli-Fachad speaks powerfully and truthfully and has immediate effect.

> And he sent her [dismembered body] into all the territories of Israel. And everyone saw and said, 'This has not happened or been seen since the days when the sons of Israel came up from the land of Egypt until this day. Apply yourselves to it. Consider. Speak.' So the sons of Israel came out, from Dan as

far as Beersheba, and the land of Gilead, and the congregation assembled as one man before the LORD at Mizpah.

(Judges 19:29–20:1)

Alice Keefe, approaching the text with attention to its semiotics, notes that on three occasions in the Hebrew Bible the rape of a woman prefigures war in Israel.[25] Within each narrative, she identifies points of similarity between the woman's situation and Israel's, and in conjunction with the well-established trope of representing Israel as a woman elsewhere, suggests that the female body is functioning as a metonym for the nation as a whole. With particular reference to Beli-Fachad, she suggests that the dismembering of the woman into twelve serves as a textual prefigurement of the fragmentation of Israel in the chapters to come.[26]

Cheryl Exum makes a similar point, asking, 'in the absence of voice, can the body speak?' and replying, 'surely [Beli-Fachad's] body is the speaking body *par excellence*. Her body, dismembered and scattered, is used semiotically to call a full-scale assembly of the Israelite tribes.'[27] Exum proceeds to argue that the woman's testimony is eclipsed by the Levite's false testimony that follows it.[28] Certainly, within the narrative, it is the Levite's words which stir the men to war, and it is his narration over her body which provides the interpretation of the events that caused it.

But this is not unproblematic to the reader. The woman has cried out powerfully for justice, just as the blood of Abel cried out for justice (Genesis 4:10). But the shape of that pursuit for justice is controlled by the man. And, as events unfold, it becomes apparent that the man's words have set in motion a dreadful chain of events that culminates in the abduction and rape of hundreds of women. In terms of their address to Israel, the woman has spoken more faithfully than the man and has done so without words. In contrast to the unreliable voice of her husband/master, Beli-Fachad speaks to Israel with a voice that is unmistakable and true. As Alice Keefe puts it, 'her narrative silence points to the eclipse of any speaking of truth in the midst of this black and bloody comedy.'[29]

Beli-Fachad speaks about Israel

Many writers have identified the semiotic effect of the treatment of women in the Hebrew Bible, and here in particular. The semiotics are generally viewed as operating at this level of the moral evaluation of Israel. For example, Tammi Schneider writes,

> The use of women as a barometer of how the Israelites are faring is most obvious when the way [Beli-Fachad] is treated is compared to Achsah, the first woman introduced in the book. [. . .] The two stand as book ends encompassing the text that leads the Israelites from the point of Achsah to that of a gang-raped woman.[30]

Some have taken this rather further, suggesting that it is the *female body* which speaks potently in this regard. For example, Susan Niditch argues, 'the woman is a visceral symbol of Israel's body politic, anticipating the way in which Israel is to be torn asunder by the civil war that follows her murder.'[31] In similar vein Jo Ann Hackett writes, 'as her body is divided, so is Israel.'[32]

We have briefly noted in Chapter 1 that one of the key *Leitmotifs* of Judges is, 'in those days there was no king in Israel, and every man did what was right in his own eyes.'[33] The book is clearly intended to critique the conduct of Israel in these premonarchical days. To this end, the book is constructed to display a dizzying catalogue of moral failures, vertiginously spiralling downwards in their depravity. (That the book is not chronologically organised is evident from the appearance in chapter 20 of Phinehas, grandson of Aaron.[34]) And at the rock bottom of this account, we meet this story of Beli-Fachad and the events that directly result from her rape and murder. The woman is being given space to speak loudly in critique of Israel's moral conduct.

Viewing this less positively, Cheryl Exum argues that Beli-Fachad is being instrumentalised; that the narrator's choice of her gang rape to illustrate the depravity of the times indicates her expendability in his eyes. The crowd's first request, that the man be put outside to them, is 'too threatening to narrate,'[35] and so Beli-Fachad is delivered up as an alternative,[36] both by the men in the narrative *and by the narrator.* After all, she deserves what is coming to her (Exum implies that the narrator thinks), so her fate is a sort of poetic justice. Nonetheless, Exum does concede that there appears to be an element of narratorial embarrassment at the woman's fate, revealed when the Israelites protest that 'such a thing has never happened or been seen.'[37]

In a paper published more or less simultaneously with Exum's book, Alice Keefe addresses this problem.

A feminist critic might read this symbolic appropriation of a woman's body as another instance of the objectification of women, as if the narrative itself were performing a double act of rape. But the semantic impact of rape as a literary trope for the dissolution of community life does not necessarily need to be read as arising out of an objectification of woman as a thing to be used. If we do not assume that women were irrelevant in the process of symbol formation in ancient Israel, either as creators of meaning or loci of value, then the possibility arises that the trope could be grounded upon *a reverence for the female body* as a site of the sacred power of life and that inscribed in the convention itself may be a respect for female subjectivity.[38]

This argument has resemblance to Judith Butler's explorations of grievability. For Butler, grief restores to us a sense of our own vulnerability (precariousness of life), both individually and in terms of a 'collective responsibility for the physical lives of one another.' What is speakable, livable, grievable, and memorable in public life is admitted to the circle of public concern. Conversely, the existence of a hierarchy of grief permits the unmourned loss of the nameless, faceless 'other,' who falls outside the normative understanding of 'human.' Grievability thus opens up space within the public sphere. 'The limit on what can be remembered is enforced in the present through what can be said and what can be heard.' Grievability is therefore both a reflection of and constitutive of public concern.

For Butler, the obituary is an important means by which grievability is publicly distributed, an act of nation-building.

> If there were to be an obituary, there would have to have been a life, a life worth noting, a life worth valuing and preserving, a life that qualifies for recognition.[39]

Butler's notion of grievability challenges us to use it to evaluate (our own and) the ancient society narrated in our chapter. Beli-Fachad's life is grievable, arguably in the minds of ancient Israel (though how much their actions are motivated by the humiliation of the Levite is moot), but more clearly in the mind of the narrator, who has given her an obituary. That he chose this story about a *pilegesh* rather than one describing an atrocity against a high-ranking wife, or a prominent man, is indicative of a surprising concern for the marginalised female *other*.

And so Beli-Fachad is given voice in moral critique of the nation. She is, perhaps, the book of Judges' other female prophet, or one of its only true judges.[40]

Beli-Fachad speaks to the modern reader

In her exploration of grievability, Judith Butler poses the following questions: 'What is real? Whose lives are real? *How might reality be remade?*'[41] In so doing, she opens up the possibility for a reparative reading. How might the *reality* of the story of Beli-Fachad propel us towards the realisation of a new reality in the 21st century? How does her voice speak to us today?

An affective reading

First, Beli-Fachad's voice speaks through the affect it engenders. Earlier we briefly considered Elaine Scarry's argument that extreme pain can render its speaking subject inarticulate. However, Scarry suggests that the artist, the narrator, can hint at this on their behalf, even if it is simply that 'the subject may enter briefly into a small corner of a literary text.'[42] And, indeed, there is such a 'small corner' in our text. At the end of her night of abuse, the *pilegesh* makes her way, crawls, we infer, to the threshold of the house where her husband/master is safely resting behind locked doors.

At dawn they let her go. And at daybreak the woman came, and fell at the door of the house where her master was until it was light. And her master arose in the morning, and he opened the door of the house and he went out to go on his way, and behold, the woman his *pilegesh* fallen at the entrance of the house, her hands on the threshold! So he said to her, 'Get up. Let's go.' But there was no reply.

The scene is pathetic; the story exercises what Denise Riley might describe as 'torsion' upon its readers;[43] it disturbs, it unsettles, it wrenches. Language, as the affect theorists show us, is capable of rupturing the barrier between our reading minds and our responsive bodies, because 'the force of violent images is *embodied* in witnesses before the witnesses judge the images according to their moral, ideological, and ethical value.'[44]

Amy Cottrill's examination of the story of Ehud's murder of Eglon in Judges 3 has shown how the use of graphic imagery, evoking olfactory participation and visceral disgust, serves a powerful narrative and rhetorical purpose.

One effect of the narrator's construction of this story is an experience of narrative triumph over the enemy, yet this particular kind of bodily violence may work on the reader in other ways as well. The reader now knows that in the book of Judges, bodies are not safe.[45]

By contrast, the narration of Beli-Fachad's tragic death is by no means so graphic. The narrator maintains a discreet distance from the abuse of the night. We do not see the spattered blood or hear the screams. But as morning comes, the narration first slows down, 'she came [. . .] she fell' (v.26) and then stops altogether in a quasi-cinematic freeze-frame that holds the shot and focusses the gaze, 'behold, the woman, his *pilegesh*, fallen at the entrance of the house, and her hand upon the threshold.' This works. It makes modern readers' flesh creep and stomachs churn.[46] Popular blogs on the subject express this:

> This story makes me feel things I don't want to feel.[47]

> A disgusting act that still offends society in every culture.[48]

> Grab some tissues or a hanky.[49]

> The stark description of the extreme sexual violence in this passage is physically nauseating for me, as a woman, to read. Although, thankfully, I've never been a victim of sexual abuse, it is all too easy for me to imagine the extreme pain, terror and degradation this poor woman went through. The text paints a picture in my head which I don't want to see.[50]

In this way, then, Beli-Fachad is able to reach through the page and disturb the modern readers of her story; the pain leaps, as it were, from her viscera to those of her readers. Her agony speaks.

As the story continues, it exercises further torsion upon the reader. Unfeelingly, the husband/master addresses the inert form. One almost imagines him nudging the prostrate body with his foot. 'Get up! Let's go.' His *pilegesh* has performed her night-time service; now it is morning, and time for him to take her on her way. But there is no answer. Is Beli-Fachad alive or dead at this stage? As Barry Webb points out, precedent in the book of Judges might suggest that if she were dead, the narrator would tell us so.[51] (Compare 19:26, in which the *pilegesh* 'falls' at the door, whereas in 5:27, Sisera 'falls dead' between Jael's feet.) Robert Polzin agrees that the narrator is being deliberately vague at this point.

> His use [. . .] of the word *wattāmot* 'and she died,' rather than, say *waḥᵃmittīhā*, 'they killed her,' does not allow us completely to dispel the suspicion that the narrator's account had engendered.[52]

The possibility of her being still alive makes his next actions even more sickening.[53]

> He came to his house and he took a knife, and he grabbed hold of his concubine and he cut her up by her bones into twelve pieces. And he sent her into all the territories of Israel.
>
> (v.29)

Beli–Fachad's husband/master's actions are callous, perhaps murderous. Every other use of the verb נתח (here translated 'cut up') in the Hebrew Bible relates to the butchering of animals, often of course carried out by the Levitical priesthood.[54] With surgical precision the narrator shows us his haste and his brutality: *He came home* [. . .] *he took* [. . .] *he seized* [. . .] *he butchered.* First, he seized her (hiphil of חזק) to put her out to the mob (v.25), now he seizes her (same verb) to send her out to Israel.

There is a further device by which the narrator drives the emotional point home to the reader. It lies in the obvious intertextuality between this passage and Genesis 19, which has been well-explored in the literature.[55] The parallels are summarised in the table that follows.

They had not yet lain down	*And they were making their heart good.*
and the men of the city, the men of Sodom, surrounded (against) the house	*But behold, men of the city, sons of Belial surrounded the house, pounding against the door.*
from old to young, all the people to the last man *And they called to Lot, saying to him* *Where are the men who came to you this night? bring them out to us that we might know them.*	*And they said to the old man, the master of the house, 'Bring out the man who has come to your house, that we might know him.'*
And Lot went out to them, to the doorway, and he shut the door behind him and he said, Please do not do evil, my brothers	*And the man, master of the house, came out to them* *and said to them, No, my brothers, please do not do evil against this man who has come to my house. Do not do this wilful sin.*
Behold, I have two daughters, who have not known a man.	*Behold my daughter, a virgin, and his concubine.*

Please let me bring them out
   to you
and you do to them according to
   the good in your eyes
Only do not do a thing to
   these men,
For they have come under the
   protection of my roof.

Please let me bring them out
   to you.
Do violence to them, and do to
   them what is good in your eyes.
But to this man, do not do this
   wicked sin.

So, when (again) the men of the city surround the house and (again) demand sexual intercourse with the male guests, the reader of the later story might reasonably expect a similar outcome to the earlier one. In the Genesis account, there is a sudden averting of danger; a divine rescue for the women offered to the mob. The visitors turn out to be angels, who blind the men of the city and enable the whole family to effect an escape. But on reading its parallel in Judges, there is no such rescue, at least, not for Beli-Fachad. (The virgin daughter disappears from view.) The narrator plays with our emotions: the danger grows, the tension builds, but we 'know' that all will be well for the woman, because we have encountered it before. And then, devastatingly, there is no sudden intervention. The woman is thrown out to the mob, and the night closes over her.

Anamnestic solidarity

A second way in which Beli-Fachad speaks to the modern reader is through the dangerous memory which she represents, and which reflects many elements of modern gender-based violence. Memory is a powerful force whereby the past can be in dialogue with the present. Refusal to forget (anamnesis) is a potent means by which the past can be redeemed and the future changed. As Walter Benjamin put it,

> [H]istory is not simply a science but also and not least a form of remembrance. What science has 'determined,' remembrance can modify. Such mindfulness can make the incomplete

(happiness) into something complete, and the complete (suffering) into something incomplete.[56]

Benjamin has been criticised for writing of women simply as objects for his own introspection, or in idealised, romanticised, ways.[57] Nonetheless, there is a helpful perspective in his view of the past, which he describes as the object of our gaze. Famously referring to Paul Klee's painting *Angelus Novus*, he describes the angel's gaze backwards at the accumulated wreckage of history at its feet, even while it is being propelled forwards into the future.[58] Benjamin urges that we should not allow this pile of wreckage that is history to remain a conglomerate, an amorphous amalgam of all the catastrophes of history. Rather, we should seize hold of a single memory as it flashes past. Or, to return to the metaphor which the painting represents, he says that we should blast a single era out of the conglomerate, and blast a single life (in particular, that of the oppressed victim) out of that era. The goal of this historical consciousness, as Benjamin puts it in typically Marxist terms, is to disrupt the false consciousness that sedates. It should subvert the hegemonic history-making of the oppressors. As Marsha Hewitt describes it, 'The present generation *redeems the past* in an act of anamnestic solidarity with all who suffered at the slaughter-bench of history.'[59]

Caroline Blyth makes a similar point about the use of modern experience to read into the gaps of the 'rape of Dinah' narrative, found in Genesis 34.

> By appealing to the witnesses and testimonies of contemporary rape survivors, by listening to the voices of women who, like the character of Dinah, have their own narratives of suffering suppressed and ignored, we may be granted insight into the significance of Dinah's own silence and the terrible suffering that lies hidden behind her voicelessness.[60]

But memory can also be transformative for the future. It can make us attentive to actions we have overlooked; it can help us to hear voices that we have not listened to. As Elisabeth Schüssler Fiorenza reminds us, history is history *for* more than history *of*.[61]

Schüssler Fiorenza's focus upon memories that empower highlights the future-orientation of memory; it has redemptive possibility.[62] While she would firmly place herself within the suspicious school of hermeneutics, this emphasis upon future orientation nonetheless makes us attentive to the reparative possibilities of memory re-examined and retold.

So we will revisit the story of Beli-Fachad once more, and allow her to address us about the present; about the multiplicity of ways that her story intersects with modern stories of gender-based violence, trafficking and abuse, and thereby acts as a vehicle for us to exercise anamnestic solidarity with her and with modern victims of gender-based violence. This opens up the question, as Judith Butler urges us, 'How might reality be remade?'[63]

The full evaluation of such points of contact would require detailed analysis of the literature on domestic violence, people trafficking, pornography, female genital mutilation, and rape, but some indicative suggestions are considered here.

Jyoti's story

On 16 December 2012,[64] a 23 year-old woman, Jyoti Singh, got onto a bus in Delhi along with a male friend, Awindra Pandey. It was 9:30 p.m. and they had been watching a film together. On their way home they had been set down by a rickshaw driver in a dangerous area and were relieved to find a bus apparently going to their destination. It was a private bus, and there were only six other people on it (all of them men), including the driver. It is unclear exactly what happened next. It may have been that the men intended to rob the couple. It may be that they were looking for a woman to rape. What is clear is that an hour and a half later, Jyoti and Awindra were thrown off the moving bus, semi-naked. Awindra had some limb fractures and bruises. Jyoti had been beaten, bitten all over her body, and raped many times, including with a hooked iron bar. Her bowel injuries were unsurvivable and she died in hospital around a fortnight later, but not before she had made a dying declaration which was used in the trial of the men eventually convicted of the atrocity. In fact, one of her three statements was made through the use of gesture rather than speech, but was nonetheless described by the judge as 'true, voluntary and consistent.'[65] Jyoti's death sparked international outrage and mass, violent protest in Delhi and beyond.

It will be clear that this story has many points of similarity with that of Beli-Fachad. Both women were assaulted in a place that should have been safe but turned out to be murderous. For Beli-Fachad, it was the Israelite city of Gibeah (vv.11–13); for Jyoti it was a bus. (Jyoti and her friend had been set down by the rickshaw driver in an unfamiliar part of town; they probably gave a sigh of relief when they were able to board a bus to their destination.) Both women were travelling with a man who might have been expected to protect them, and who managed to survive the night's events, when the women didn't.[66] Both women were raped and abused by night, then discarded (v.25). Both women's murders evoked widespread outrage and violent reaction (chapters 20–21). Both women have been blamed for the assault that killed them.[67]

Indian law prohibits the naming of victims of sexual violence. Until Jyoti's anonymity was waived by her family, the Indian press dubbed her Nirbhaya, meaning fearless; a tribute, I think, to the courageous way in which she resisted her attackers, fought for life for a fortnight afterwards, and made a dying declaration which testified powerfully after her death. For these reasons, because of her enduring voice and her silent but powerful testimony, I chose the Hebrew translation of 'Nirbhaya' as the name for the woman of the biblical story: Beli-Fachad, Without-Fear.

Other stories

Jyoti's story is one of many thousands which resonate with Judges 19. Broadly, they share the themes of commodification, depersonalisation, instrumentalisation, invisibility, trafficking, silence, the violence of women being subordinated to other (often male) concerns, the 'unrapeability' myth, and the rape of women as an assault against men.

COMMODIFICATION AND DEPERSONALISATION

Yani Yoo, writing in *Semeia* in 1997, compares the story of Judges 19–21 with the situation of Korean 'comfort women' in the first half of the 20th century.[68] She identifies multiple similarities between the narrative in Judges 19 and the experience of these women; in particular, their shared experience of comfortlessness and the ways in which they were commodified, depersonalised, and silenced.

With relation to commodification and depersonalisation, Yoo describes how the 'comfort women' were listed on inventories along with military supplies and were shipped with the munitions. They were simply viewed as 'things which had genitals.'[69] So is Beli-Fachad. Her husband/master's indifference to her on the morning after her assault is indicative of that. She has performed her night-time duty; now it is time for them to be on their way.

The depersonalisation of trafficked people is a noticeable feature in an interview with Dina, a Khmer orphan who got into debt for overdue rent and tuition fee payments, and was consequently sex-trafficked at the age of seventeen:

> I want you to remember we are not 'problems,' we are not ani-
> mals, we are not viruses, we are not garbage. We are flesh, skin
> and bones; we have a heart, and we have feelings. We are a sister
> to someone, a daughter, a granddaughter. We are people, we are
> women, and we want to be treated with respect, dignity. And
> we want rights like the rest of you enjoy.[70]

A similar description of women involved in violent pornography is offered by Robert Jensen. 'Increasingly, women in pornography are not people having sex but bodies upon which sexual activities of increasing cruelty are played out.'[71]

The instrumentalisation of Beli-Fachad by her husband/master also has disturbing resonances with much more recent events. It is striking that he uses her at night, in this instance by making use of her to deflect the threat against his own person, and then expects her to continue to serve him in the daytime [Get up! Let's go!' (19:28)]. Similar stories are recorded of enslaved women working in the house or field all day and then being used for sexual purposes at night.[72] In her book *The Industrial Vagina*, Sheila Jeffreys itemises many ways in which women's bodies are instrumentalised for others' financial gain.[73]

Comparing elements of the biblical story with modern-day sex trafficking, Mitzi Smith refers to the 'invisibility' of the trafficked person, relating it to Beli-Fachad:

> The concubine's victimization remains invisible to us because what we see, or don't see, we declare as normal – her victimization is concealed behind ideas of patriarchal normalcy. [...] The concubine ceases to exist, in the story, until the Levite reclaims her from her father's house. In her father's house she lives in a state of liminality.[74]

Indeed, the invisibility of the other woman in the story, the old man's daughter, is even more marked. Viewed by her father as a commodity in the same way as Beli-Fachad is, she appears to escape by melting into the background, making herself even more invisible. Lyrae Van Clief-Stefanon's stunning poem, 'The Daughter and the Concubine from the Nineteenth Chapter of Judges Consider and Speak Their Minds,' picks up on the virgin daughter's part in the story with great sensitivity.[75]

TRAFFICKING

Mitzi Smith strengthens our understanding of the links between sex trafficking and the biblical story by drawing attention to the 'travelling' motif within the story; Beli-Fachad is being conveyed, with no agency of her own, from her father's house to her husband/master's. In a similar way,

> Modern-day sex-trafficking depends on the ability of the victim's predators to transport her across geographical boundaries; to remove her permanently or temporarily from her normal geographic surroundings.[76]

Chuck Pitt finds further links between modern trafficking and the narrative through the motif of protector-as-procurer, identified in

Judges 19 by Phyllis Trible.[77] Trible points out that Beli-Fachad's master/husband, who has a duty of care towards her, fails to protect her; and her host, who also has a duty of care, actively pimps her out for the safety of his male guest. Pitt links this to the way that many modern victims of trafficking are first 'befriended' by their pimps and traffickers: they are first 'boyfriend,' then pimp.[78]

SILENCE

The silence of Beli-Fachad within the narrative resonates with many other modern readers. Writing of child sexual abuse, David Garber and Daniel Stallings draw parallels between the silencing of modern victims of abuse and that of the *pilegesh*:

> Like the Levite's concubine, victims of sex trafficking have been afforded no voice in retaliation for the heinous actions taken against them. Likewise, the church has largely been unsuccessful in providing a voice for these who have been the victims of such horrible brutality.
>
> If, however, [the *pilegesh*] had a voice that would be heard – if her voice counted – would she not have used it? If she could have prevented her suffering and death, would she not have done so? What if someone had offered to speak on her behalf? Would she have refused that hospitality?[79]

VIOLENCE AGAINST WOMEN SUBORDINATED TO OTHER CONCERNS

Reading Judges 19 as the story of a young woman whose departure to her father is a flight from domestic violence, Marie Fortune notices how the final act of violation against her is deflected by the Levite and his hearers into a narrative of threatened violence against his own person and actual damage to his own property. In similar vein Tammi Schneider shows how the female violence becomes subsumed by the masculine *casus belli*,

> While it is not surprising that the man would hide any culpability he had in the rape and murder of this woman, it is important for the sake of the cause. The Levite instigated a civil war.[80]

Fortune comments that this account in Judges reflects the modern reluctance to name violence against women as wrong or sinful. She gives the example of a group of church members at a conference about pornography, who were shown a short (fictional) video which portrayed the brutal murder of a naked woman. Viewers' responses reflected anger at the nakedness and erotic imagery but not at the portrayed violence against the woman. Fortune asks:

> Why is it that women's sexuality is so offensive in the church but women's victimization is not? Why does the church still [. . .] name sexuality as sin and at the same time, hesitate to name violence against women and children a sin?[81]

UNRAPEABILITY

Few commentators have noted the intersectional elements of oppression within the narrative.[82] The Levite and his entourage are *gerim*, sojourners (19:1), staying at the house of another *ger*, which appears to be what singles them out for the hostile attention of the men of the town.[83] The female traveller is not simply a woman – itself a disadvantage in a patriarchal society – but is a *pilegesh*. Whether, as we have considered previously, this here refers to her as a concubine; a second wife; or existing within some other, irregular marital arrangement, she is clearly in an underclass. She is neither a first wife nor a high-ranking woman. This compounds the societal inequalities that are stacked up against her and lays her open to high-handed usage by not only her husband/master, but by her host, too (v.24). Although it seems to be clear that the ancient understanding of 'rape' is very different from our own,[84] the legal terminology need not detain us here. It appears that these intersectional factors combine to make Beli-Fachad 'fair game' for the treatment that she receives at the hands of her husband/master, and – in the eyes of the men of the town – the treatment that they give her.

Such a situation bears points of similarity to modern rape myths, which regard certain women – typically sex workers or women of a minority ethnic origin – as 'unrapeable.' This is not to say that these women are untouchable, but that in certain portions of the popular imagination, sexual assault of these women does not constitute 'rape,' and therefore, the women are 'fair game.'[85] For example, consider the rape myth that you can't rape a sex worker, it's just shoplifting.[86] Further, in the United Kingdom, it was not until 1991 that marital rape was regarded as a criminal act; in other words, until 1991, wives were (by their husbands) unrapeable. There remain many countries in the world today where this continues to be the case.

RAPE OF WOMEN AS ASSAULT ON MEN

Another point of contact between the biblical story and modern sexual violence lies in the rape of women to shame or humiliate men. It is clear that the intentions of the 'sons of Belial' who surround the house are to humiliate and shame the men. James Harding has persuasively argued that rape is always about gendered symbolic violence, rather than about sexual desire. In this way the threatened rape against the Levite and the actual rape of the woman are not contrasted alternatives ('heterosexual' rape substituted for 'homosexual' rape), but one and the same action.

> The threat to rape the Levite man on the one hand, and the physical rape of the [woman] on the other [. . .] reflect a single structure of thought, namely masculine domination.[87]

This might be compared with the modern use of male rape to humiliate and dominate, such as, for example, the 2017 report of the systematic use of male rape in Libya as a weapon of war.[88] In similar ways, systematic female rape has been used as a weapon of war or as an act of genocide, in part to humiliate the male members of the tribe or nation. For example, Serbian men assaulting Muslim women in the 'rape camps' of the Yugoslavian war are said to have shouted 'death to all Turkish sperm.'[89] Or, in a smaller-scale but widely reported example, the 2018 abduction, rape, and murder of an 8-year-old girl in the Jammu and Kashmir state of India was widely understood to have been conducted by Hindu men to drive away a Muslim nomadic tribe of which she was a part.[90]

So Beli-Fachad's voice does continue to speak. Even though she has no speech her voice is heard, just as Jyoti Singh's voice was heard through her dying declaration given in gesture. Beli-Fachad's story is, to appropriate the words of Elisabeth Schüssler Fiorenza, a dangerous memory, a historical artefact that neither time nor patriarchy has succeeded in eroding.[91] True, it is situated within a patriarchal text and therefore is a product of male ideas about women. Clearly it reflects the military and political concerns of its authors.[92] But its retelling constitutes a determined resistance to historical amnesia and opens up redemptive possibilities. It brings us into anamnestic solidarity with the dead woman who is not now in need of redemption but whose modern readers may be.

Beli-Fachad is not silent in the 21st century, and she does not lack agency here. She has reached through the pages and seized our guts, twisting them to her purpose, calling our attention to her plight. She then urges us to notice the many points of comparison between her story and those of millions of women today. Her voice is loud and pressing and urges transformation.

Notes

1 Exum, *Fragmented Women*.
2 This classic example is explored in much more detail in J. L. Austin, *How to Do Things with Words*, 2nd ed. (Cambridge: Harvard University Press, 1962), 25–39.
3 This is using the term 'thick descriptions' in a different way than I did in the introduction.
4 Kit Barker, *Imprecation as Divine Discourse: Speech Act Theory, Dual Authorship and Theological Interpretation,* Journal of Theological Interpretation Supplement 16 (Winona Lake: Eisenbrauns, 2016); Vern Sheridan Poythress, "Canon and Speech Act: Limitations in Speech-act Theory, with Implications for a Putative Theory of Canonical Speech Acts," *Westminster Theological Journal* 70 (2008): 337–54.
5 This is adapted from the excellent summary found in Barker, *Imprecation,* 82–89.
6 These are: the response of tribal Israel, the editor of the book of Judges, the shapers of the canon, the prophets, the rest of scripture, and the reader.
7 Barry Webb describes the hospitality as 'farcical.' Webb, *The Book of Judges,* 459.
8 For example, both Alberto Soggin and Daniel Block assert that the MT of this verse makes no sense as it stands. Soggin, *Judges,* 287; Block, *Judges, Ruth,* 531 FN 227.
9 The Masoretes do not indicate any discomfort with this phrase, as they offer no *ketiv-qere*. None of the extant Hebrew texts has בֵּיתִי (my house). BHQ has a fairly lengthy textual note, concluding that it is preferable to leave the MT text as it stands. Natalio Fernández Marcos, *Biblical Hebraica:*

Quinta editione cum apparatu critic novis curis elabaorato (Stuttgart: Deutsche Bibelgesellschaft, 2011), 108. This is *contra* Emmanuel Tov, *Textual Criticism of the Hebrew (Bible Second revised edition)* (Minneapolis: Fortress, 2001), 256–57.

10 Meir Sternberg, *The Poetics of Biblical Narrative: Ideological Literature and the Drama of Reading* (Bloomington: Indiana University Press, 1985), 189–230.

11 Webb, *The Book of Judges*, 475.

12 Exum, *Fragmented Women*, 186.

13 Stuart Lasine, "Guest and Host in Judges 19: Lot's Hospitality in an Inverted World," *Journal for the Study of the Old Testament* 29 (1984): 49. However, Lasine's description of the absurdity within the narrative goes perhaps too far. He considers that the parodic execration of the man inhibits our sympathy for the woman, a view I shall dispute in a following section. He also considers that the Levite's actions are 'so bizarre that they burst the category of tragic villainy.' Sadly, as we shall see in the extended comparison of the narrative with modern sexual violence, his actions are all-too-often replicated in the modern world.

14 For example, David Moster says, 'the Levite is never criticised for his behavior.' David Z. Moster, "The Levite of Judges 19–21," *Journal of Biblical Literature* 134, no. 4 (2015): 728.

15 Bal, *Death and Dissymmetry*.

16 Bal, *Death and Dissymmetry*, 23.

17 Bal, *Death and Dissymmetry*, 126.

18 T. Huckin, "Textual Silence and the Discourse of Homelessness," *Discourse Society* 13 (2002): 347–72.

19 Exum, *Fragmented Women*, 197.

20 Exum, *Fragmented Women*, 194.

21 Exum, *Fragmented Women*, 196.

22 Catharine A. MacKinnon and Andrea Dworkin, "Minneapolis Ordinance, 1983," in *In Harm's Way: The Pornography Civil Rights Hearings* (Cambridge: Harvard University Press, 1997), 426–31.

23 Exum, *Fragmented Women*, 197.

24 Elaine Scarry, *The Body in Pain: The Making and Unmaking of the World* (Oxford: Oxford University Press, 1985), 366.

25 Alice A. Keefe, "Rapes of Women, Wars of Men," *Semeia* 61 (1993): 79–97. The three instances that Keefe refers to are the rape of Dinah (Genesis 34), Beli-Fachad, and Tamar (2 Samuel 13). I am grateful to my student Rhiannon Gray for directing my attention to this paper.

26 Keefe, "Rapes of Women," 79–97. *Contra* this view, see Amit, *The Art of Editing*, 337–40.

27 Exum, *Fragmented Women*, 190–91.

28 A similar point is made in Fewell and Gun, *Gender, Power, and Promise*, 135.

29 Keefe, "Rapes of Women," 92.

30 Schneider, *Judges*, 246.

31 Susan Niditch, *Judges: A Commentary* (Louisville: John Knox Press, 2008), 194.

32 Jo Ann Hackett, "Violence and Women's Lives in the Book of Judges," *Interpretation* (October 2004): 362.

33 On Judges as an apologia for the Davidic kingship see A. E. Cundall, "Judges – An Apology for the Monarchy?" *Expository Times* 81 (1969–70): 178–81. For a contrary view, see Cynthia Edenburg, *Dismembering the Whole: Composition and Purpose of Judges 19–21* (Atlanta: SBL Press, 2016).

34 This has been explored in detail in David H. Beldman, "The Completion of Judges: Strategies of Ending in Judges 17–21" (unpublished PhD thesis, University of Bristol, 2013). I am grateful to Dr. Peter Hatton for drawing my attention to this.

35 Exum, *Fragmented Women,* 183.

36 It is striking that three of the murdered women of Judges, and the 400 women abducted from Shiloh, are all regarded as fungible; that is, they are all potentially exchangeable with someone else. The sister of Samson's wife was offered as an acceptable exchange for her by their father, before the wife (and the father) are burned to death by the Philistines (Judges 15:2,5). Jephthah's daughter represents the one who happened to come first out of the house on her father's return, but it could easily have been someone else who suffered her fate (Judges 11:30–40). Beli-Fachad, in our passage, is offered as a fungible item instead of her husband/master. And the 400 abducted women of Judges 21 are taken as fungible substitutes for the wives that the people of Israel would otherwise have provided for the men of Benjamin.

37 Judges 19:30; Exum, *Fragmented Women,* 187.

38 Keefe, "Rapes of Women," 88 (emphasis added).

39 Judith Butler, *Precarious Life: The Powers of Mourning and Violence* (London: Verso, 2004), 34.

40 After Deborah, and perhaps, by a similar argument to the one I have used here, the daughter of Jephthah.

41 Butler, *Precarious Life,* 33 (emphasis added).

42 Scarry, *Body in Pain,* 11.

43 Denise Riley, *Impersonal Passion: Language as Affect* (Durham: Duke University Press, 2005), 3.

44 Amy C. Cottrill, "A Reading of Ehud and Jael Through the Lens of Affect Theory," *Biblical Interpretation* 22, no. 4–5 (2014): 437 (emphasis added).

45 Cottrill, "A Reading of Ehud and Jael," 443.

46 I am reminded of the fingernail marks on the walls of the gas chamber in Auschwitz, to which our gaze is also drawn, which serve as a sort of metonymical witness to the anguish we did not see.

47 Accessed June 19, 2019, https://thewholedangthing.wordpress.com/2012/11/15/judges-19-the-levites-concubine/.

48 Accessed June 19, 2019, https://godswordtowomen.org/walford.htm.

49 Accessed June 19, 2019, https://meetinggodinthemargin.com/2017/06/28/first-reading-of-judges-19-the-levites-concubine/.

50 'Philippa,' Comment on this blog post, accessed June 19, 2019, www.psephizo.com/biblical-studies/can-we-preach-on-the-texts-of-terror/.

51 Webb, *The Book of Judges,* 472.

52 Robert Polzin, *Moses and the Deuteronomist: A Literary Study of the Deuteronomic History* (New York: Seabury Press, 1980), 201.

53 Meir Sternberg uses this as a cardinal example of 'gapping' in narrative; that is, the deliberate omission by the narrator of information which the reader seeks, causing the reader to draw inferences, read imaginatively, and play with ambiguous possibilities. Sternberg, *Poetics,* 238–39.

54 Ex. 29:17; Lev. 16:12; 8:20; 1Sam. 11:7; 1 Kgs 18:23, 33.

55 The direction of the literary dependency has been well-discussed and remains unclear. (See, for example, Butler, *Judges,* 412–13; Lasine, "Guest and Host," 37–59; Niditch, *Judges,* 192; Daniel I. Block, "Echo Narrative Technique in Hebrew Literature: A Study in Judges 19," *Westminster Theological Journal* 52, no. 2 (1990): 325–41.) I have argued elsewhere (Helen Paynter, *Reduced Laughter: Seriocomic Features and Their Functions in the Book of Kings* (Leiden: Brill, 2016), 8) that, since the Hebrew narratives appear to have had a long pre-textual oral tradition, it is not necessary to postulate a single pre-text and a single dependent text, but rather that texts can develop in conversation with one another in the oral stage of the tradition.

56 Walter Benjamin, *The Arcades Project,* trans. Howard Eiland and Kevin McLaughlin (Cambridge: Harvard University Press, 1999), 471.

57 Marsha Hewitt, "The Redemptive Power of Memory: Walter Benjamin and Elisabeth Schüssler Fiorenza," *Journal of Feminist Studies in Religion* 10, no. 1 (1994): 73–89.

58 Walter Benjamin, *On the Concept of History Gesammelte Schriften I.2* (1974), trans. Dennis Redmond, accessed July 16, 2019, www.arts.yorku.ca/soci/barent/wp-content/uploads/2008/10/benjaminconcept_of_history1.pdf.

59 Hewitt, "Redemptive Power," 77.

60 Blyth, "Terrible Silence, Eternal Silence," 499.

61 Elisabeth Schüssler Fiorenza, *Bread Not Stone: The Challenge of Feminist Biblical Interpretation* (Boston: Beacon Press, 1984), 93–115.

62 Elisabeth Schüssler Fiorenza, *In Memory of Her: A Feminist Theological Reconstruction of Christian Origins* (New York: Crossroad, 1990), 31.

63 Butler, *Precarious Life,* 33 (emphasis added).

64 This story has been reconstructed from multiple media sources and is a matter of public record.

65 Press Trust of India, *Nirbhaya's Declarations by Hand Gestures "True, Consistent": Top Court,* accessed July 22, 2019, www.ndtv.com/india-news/nirbhayas-dying-declarations-made-by-hand-gestures-were-true-consistent-supreme-court-1880688.

66 I am not wishing to imply that Awindra Pandey was in any way complicit in the events of the evening, simply that his injuries were far less extensive that the woman's.

67 We saw in Chapter 2 some examples where Beli-Fachad has been blamed for her rape and death. Similarly, one of Jyoti's attackers has blamed her for her death. He was reported as making the following comments: 'A decent girl won't roam around at nine o'clock at night. [. . .] A girl is far more responsible for rape than a boy. Boys and girls are not equal. [. . .] Housework and housekeeping is for girls, not roaming in discos and bars

at night doing wrong things, wearing wrong clothes. [. . .] When being raped, she shouldn't fight back. [. . .] She should just be silent and allow the rape. Then they'd have dropped her off after doing her and only hit the boy.' He also said that if his sister or daughter 'disgraced herself' by being seen with a man, he would go 'to my farmhouse, and in front of my entire family, I would put petrol on her and set her alight.' Lizzie Dearden, "Delhi Bus Rapist Blames Dead Victim for Attack Because 'Girls Are Responsible for Rape," *The Independent*, March 2, 2015, accessed July 22, 2019, www.independent.co.uk/news/world/asia/delhi-bus-rapist-blames-dead-victim-for-attack-because-girls-are-responsible-for-rape-10079894.html.

68 Yani Yoo, "Han-laden Women: Korean 'Comfort Women' and Women in Judges 19–21," *Semeia* 78 (1997): 37.

69 Yoo, "Han-laden Women," 42.

70 Kevin Bales and Zoe Trodd, eds., *To Plead Our Own Cause: Personal Stories by Today's Slaves* (Ithaca: Cornell, 2008), 103.

71 Quoted in Chris Hedges, *Empire of Illusion: The End of Literacy and the Triumph of Spectacle* (New York: Nation, 2009), 61.

72 Andrea H. Livesey, "'Race, Slavery, and the Expression of Sexual Violence,' in *The Octoroon*, ed. Louisa Picquet," *American Nineteenth Century History* 193 (2018): 267–88.

73 Sheila Jeffreys, *The Industrial Vagina: The Political Economy of the Global Sex Trade* (London: Routledge, 2009).

74 Mitzi J. Smith, "Reading the Story of the Levite's Concubine Through the Lens of Modern-Day Sex Trafficking," *Ashland Theological Journal* 41 (2009): 23–24.

75 Lyrae Van Clief-Stefanon, Black Swan, Pitt Poetry Series (Pittsburgh: University of Pittsburgh Press, 2002), 31–36.

76 Smith, "Reading the Story," 22.

77 Trible, *Texts of Terror*, 74.

78 Chuck Pitts, "Judges 19 as a Paradigm for Understanding and Responding to Human Trafficking," *Priscilla Papers* 29, no. 4 (2015): 5.

79 David G. Garber Jr. and Daniel Stallings, "Awakening Desire Before It Is Season: Reading Biblical Texts in Response to the Sexual Exploitation of Children," *Review & Expositor* 105, no. 3 (2008): 466.

80 Schneider, *Judges*, 268.

81 Marie M. Fortune, "The Nature of Abuse," *Pastoral Psychology* 41, no. 5 (1993): 286.

82 'Intersectionality' is a term first used by Kimberle Crenshaw to describe a multi-axis framework for describing oppression and discrimination; for example, the intersecting roles of race and gender. See Kimberle Williams Crenshaw, "Demarginalizing the Intersection of Race and Sex: A Black Feminist Critique of Antidiscrimination Doctrine, Feminist Theory and Antiracist Politics," *University of Chicago Legal Forum* (1989): 139–67.

83 For a discussion of the marginalised status of the Levite, see Moster, "The Levite of Judges 19–21," 721–30.

84 Susan Brownmiller's definition of modern female rape is, 'if a woman chooses not to have intercourse with a specific man and the man chooses

to proceed against her will' (Brownmiller, *Against our Will*, 18). However, even in modern situations, this definition is problematic. It appears to exclude penetration with an object rather than a penis, oral penetration, and the situation where consent is not actively refused (e.g. an unconscious woman). In the ancient world, this definition is even more problematic, as Leah Schulte has shown. [Leah Rediger Schulte, *The Absence of God in Biblical Rape Narratives* (Philadelphia: Fortress Press, 2017), 1–32.] Schulte argues that, in the biblical understanding, the victim of the rape is the male family member who will lose financially from the loss of the girl's virginity. Thus, rape is not unsolicited sexual activity, but is unauthorised sexual activity. This means that a woman's male protectors have some culpability when she is raped. [Esther Fuchs, *Sexual Politics in the Biblical Narrative: Reading the Hebrew Bible as a Woman* (London: A&C Black, 2003), 200–24.] The ambiguity is compounded by the fact that there is no clear Hebrew word for 'rape' found in the Hebrew Bible. (See also Sandie Gravett, "Reading 'Rape' in the Hebrew Bible: A Consideration of Language," *Journal for the Study of the Old Testament* 28, no. 3 (2004): 279–99.) Schulte also draws attention to the aftermath of a biblical rape. The victim of a biblical rape (if she survives) is 'desolate' (2 Samuel 13:20) because she is unmarriageable; thus, the focus of the biblical text is broader than attention to the act itself.

85 Jody Miller and Martin D. Schwartz, "Rape Myths and Violence Against Street Prostitutes," *Deviant Behavior* 16, no. 1 (1995): 1–23; Roxanne Donovan and Michelle Williams, "Living at the Intersection: The Effects of Racism and Sexism on Black Rape Survivors," *Women & Therapy* 25, no. 3–4 (2002): 95–105.

86 I am unable to trace the source of this quotation, but it is commonly referred to as something that 'people say.' See, for example, accessed July 22, 2019, https://junkee.com/sex-work-analogy-prostitute-slur/43410.

87 James Harding, "Homophobia and Masculine Domination in Judges 19–21," *The Bible and Critical Theory* 12, no. 2 (2016): 42. Harding is here building upon the work of Pierre Bourdieu, *Masculine Domination,* trans. Richard Nice (Stanford: Stanford University Press, 2001).

88 Accessed June 21, 2019, www.theguardian.com/world/2017/nov/03/revealed-male-used-systematically-in-libya-as-instrument-of-war.

89 Samuel Totten, Paul Robert Bartrop, and Steven L. Jacobs, *Dictionary of Genocide: Volume 1. ABC-CLIO* (London: Greenwood, 2008), 160.

90 See, for example, the report in the Daily Telegraph, accessed June 21, 2019, www.telegraph.co.uk/news/2019/06/10/six-hindu-men-convictedover-rape-murder-muslim-girl-8-case-fanned/.

91 Schüssler Fiorenza, *Bread Not Stone,* 109.

92 Bal, *Death and Dissymmetry,* 5.

Conclusion

My stated aim at the outset of this investigation was to explore whether a reparative hermeneutic enables us to view the story of the rape, murder, and dismemberment of Beli-Fachad without suspicion but still without misogyny. Reparative readings, as Sedgwick conceived them, do not deny the prevalent ideologies but, rather, choose not to foreclose the way that the text might be found to exist within them.

In particular, we have paid attention to the levels of communication performed by the text and have made the deliberate choice not to collapse the view of the narrator into the view of any of the characters in the narrative. Thus it is possible to consider separately the treatment and subjectivity given to Beli-Fachad by the characters with whom she interacts, by the narrator, and – by extension of this logic – by the commentators.

Cheryl Exum's argument that Beli-Fachad is 'raped by the pen' of the narrator is based upon six perceived injustices perpetrated against her: anonymity, character assassination, narrative punishment, reward of the Levite, representation of the woman as a chaotic force, and pornographic objectification. I have commented on each of these, but it might be appropriate here to draw the strands of my argument together.

With regard to anonymity, I have produced evidence that it is not *necessarily* obliterative, and that it can be used as a narrative device to exemplify, and thus paradoxically prioritise, the individual and the matters to which she bears witness.

We have discussed at some length the representation of Beli-Fachad's character within the narrative and have concluded that there is some ambiguity as to what she may or may not be said to have done. Admittedly, much of this ambiguity lies in the interplay between textual variants, but this may point both to a multiplicity of oral traditions in the pre-textual period or alongside the earliest texts.[1] And even within the most critical textual variant – the Hebrew one – there is reason to doubt the harshest interpretations. Moreover, the *possibility* of sexual transgression opens up a moral agency that is often denied to the woman.

With regard to the related concern about Beli-Fachad receiving narrative punishment, there is indeed reason to suspect that the Levite's willingness to sacrifice his *pilegesh* relates to the – real or perceived – trouble she has caused him. But does the narrator likewise sacrifice her? I have argued that this is much less evident; indeed, that the narrative punishment works in quite the opposite direction, as we shall see shortly.

In terms of the Levite being 'rewarded' for his unreliable account of events, we have considered the mismatch between his speech and actions and what this reveals about his character. The unreliable speech functions more as a character critique than as a literary vehicle for reward. True, his deceitful words do motivate the nation to military action, but when the catastrophic outcome of that military action is manifest, it seems perverse to regard this as a reward in any sense. The Levite gains nothing –nor, for that matter, does anyone else. And is the woman perceived as a 'chaotic' force within the nation? It would be fairer, perhaps, to see the chaotic forces at play when the 'sons of Belial' get to work in the darkness.

Finally, I have argued that the focus which the narrator places upon the hands of the bloodied and violated woman as she lies upon the threshold is better understood as empathetic than pornographic.

But there is another pen – or rather, a thousand more pens – by which Beli-Fachad can be raped and has been raped.[2] These are the pens of the traditional commentators who have, among them, committed every one of the sins that Exum has outlined. If rape is a denial of subjectivity, then Beli-Fachad has indeed been raped. She has been ignored, marginalised, and victim-shamed. Her character has been smeared. She has been viewed as the cause of trouble; her suffering has been celebrated as the will of God.

Does such a statement represent a paranoid reading *of* the commentators? Should I not be seeking a more generous, optimistic, reparative reading? Perhaps when two texts (the biblical one and the comment upon it) appear to be in moral and ideological tension, a reparative reading of the one will necessitate a paranoid reading of the other.

But if the text is not actually *raping* Beli-Fachad, is it at least indifferent to her, as Trible asserts? If we are to be attentive readers, we need to notice comment that is made by a text at an implicit level as well as explicit comment. If we are to be reparative readers, we should read with hope.

Meir Sternberg argues that rape is taken extremely seriously by the Hebrew Bible as a whole.[3] Rapists face narrative consequences (here, *contra* Exum, he would view the civil war as punishment, not reward). From the Deuteronomic period onwards, rape of a betrothed woman is punishable by death, a more stringent punishment even than murder, since within law and narrative murderers can at times receive 'less than their legal deserts.'[4] In contrast, he says, 'every "abuser" in the plot (the Gibeah gang, Amnon, as well as Shechem) falls under the charge of "outrage in Israel" and dies by the sword.'[5] Sternberg has here taken a rather narrow view of biblical rape, in my view, as the experience of Hagar, Bilhah and Zilpah, and Esther (among others) should probably also be included. Nevertheless, Sternberg's point is a reasonable generalisation and in the case of Beli-Fachad it holds.[6]

More than this, however, Sternberg argues in typically bombastic style that narrative silence is not complicity. To say otherwise is nonsensical:

> By [such] logic, the absence of the narrator's overt judgment would indicate free judgment on Ham's seeing the nakedness of his father, on the Israelite's worship of the golden calf, on David's adultery with Bathsheba followed by her widowing, on Jezebel's judicial murder of Naboth. [Such a reader] has lost his/her moral mearings, suddenly transported into a

world of such fantastic permissiveness that every crime turns neutral or enjoys the benefit of doubt unless proclaimed criminal.[7]

By means of the sharp critique of the Levite, and by means of the narrative consequences that ensue, the narrator's judgment is handed down. This is indeed an 'outrage in Israel.'

There are two contrasting dangers faced by someone charged with the responsibility of reporting, describing, or writing histories of violence. The first is to omit it, suppress it, or air-brush it out of history and memory. The second danger is to endorse, normalise, or glorify the violence. Our narrator has been charged with both wrongs. Can he be exonerated of either, or both?

The charge of obliteration does not really stand up to scrutiny. We have argued for the subjectivity of Beli-Fachad within the narrative, at various levels of communication. And the fact that the violence against her is discussed and written about, whether deplored or lauded, highlights that the act has not been air-brushed out of the historical record. The application of Judith Butler's challenge of grievability shows us that the inclusion of Beli-Fachad's story makes a potent comment about her value within the eyes of the narrator (and of the textual curators who have preserved her story). And the use of her story to condemn the moral decline of the nation elevates it further.

Far from these last chapters deserving excision, their role in bringing the themes of the book to climax should be appreciated. As Robert Polzin says:

> Since we are at the finale of our stories about Israel's exploits during the period of the judges, we would expect that it provide us with a fitting climax to the major themes so brilliantly worked out by the Deuteronomist in the course of this book, and we are not disappointed. If the book's first chapter began with an effective psychological portrait of the process whereby Israel, after Joshua's death, progressively went from certainty to confusion concerning the high expectations of victory

guaranteed her by a Mosaic covenant, the books finale now completes with a flourish the paradoxical picture of confusion within certainty, obscurity in clarity, that has occupied its pages from the start.[8]

Whether with Bal we attend to the coherent and counter-coherent themes of male/female concerns; political affairs/domestic affairs, or we follow the more standard line that the themes within the text are of the need for a Davidic king and the cohesion of Israel, all of these are brought to fitting conclusion and climax in these closing scenes of the biblical account.

The interpretation I here offer, reaching towards a reparative reading, shows that the text neither obliterates the *pilegesh* (in contrast to the ways that many of her male readers have done) nor glamorises the violence against her, but rather views her with tenderness. Elisabeth Schüssler Fiorenza says of the New Testament, 'feminist critical hermeneutics must test whether and how much some biblical translations contain emancipatory elements that have transcended critically their cultural patriarchal contexts.'[9] A reparative reading of this much more ancient narrative against its cultural patriarchal background likewise reveals emancipatory elements.

However, I do not intend this reparative reading to become a totalising interpretation of this text. It should, rather, remain in creative dialogue with the suspicious readings of Bal, Exum, Trible and others. As we saw in Chapter 3, Jennifer Knust argues that neither paranoid nor reparative readings can wholly stand alone. Rather, they should be held together in creative dialogue. A reparative reading is not a denial of the underlying patriarchy represented within the text. As Robyn Wiegman says,

> The paranoid position is not the sole scene in which the subject encounters anxiety and aggression; both the paranoid and the reparative positions are responses to the same environmental conditions of ambivalence, risk, and dependence.[10]

In fact, as we have seen, there are emancipatory or reparative elements within each of the suspicious readings that we considered earlier.

This female-centred reparative reading should also remain in creative dialogue with those readings which focus upon the theological and political themes that the narrative is developing. The story is too rich and deep and complex to be collapsed into a single, though legitimate, illocution. Rather, by foregrounding the *pilegesh*, this reading attempts to bring her into dialogue with those more traditional commentators, and to restore what has often been an imbalance in the representation of the text.

We have seen that the narrative of the Levite's wife is deeply embedded within what we might nowadays call a rape culture. However, the case has here been made that the narrator distantiates himself from this. Those who seek the divine voice in the narrative may choose to draw their own conclusions from this critical distantiation between the narrator and the events he is describing.

Eve Sedgwick's appeal for reparative readings calls for the reader to uncover good surprises within the text. For Beli-Fachad the *pilegesh*, whose disjointed bones have long turned to dust in the soil of Israel, there can be no good surprises. But for Beli-Fachad the judge of the covenant people of God; for Beli-Fachad the foremother of those raped and discarded women who come after her; for Beli-Fachad who still speaks to us prophetically today, there may yet be good surprises in store.

Notes

1 David Carr, *The Formation of the Hebrew Bible: A New Reconstruction* (Oxford: Oxford University Press, 2011).

2 Exum refers to this in passing: Exum, *Fragmented Women*, 171.

3 A similar point is made by Susanne Scholz. '[T]he existence of so many rape texts in the Hebrew Bible establishes this literature's inherent "morality." It does not endorse violence and bloodthirstiness.' Scholz, *Sacred Witness*, 211.

4 Meir Sternberg, "'Biblical Poetics and Sexual Politics: From Reading to Counterreading," *Journal of Biblical Literature* 111 (1992): 474.

5 Sternberg, "Biblical Poetics and Sexual Politics," 474.

6 This argument is supported by the work of Pamela Reis, who argues that rather than glorifying or normalising the violence against her, the narrative distances itself from the actions in three ways: men are not privileged in the narrative but rather their actions are critiqued, the author shows empathy

towards the *pilegesh*, the guilty receive narrative punishment. Reis, "The Levite's Concubine," 126. I do, however, take issue with Reis's oblique claim to making an objective reading of the text, 'I am a feminist. But I hew to the text, not to ideology' (p. 125).

7 Sternberg, "Biblical Poetics and Sexual Politics," 473–74.
8 Polzin, *Moses and the Deuteronomist*, 200.
9 Schüssler Fiorenza, *In Memory of Her*, 33.
10 Wiegman, *The Times We're in*, 17.

Works consulted

Ahmed, Sara. *The Promise of Happiness.* Durham: Duke University Press, 2010.

Alter, Robert. *The Art of Biblical Narrative.* London: George Allen & Unwin, 1981.

Amit, Yairah. *The Book of Judges: The Art of Editing.* Translated by Jonathan Chipman. Leiden: Brill, 1999.

Austin, J. L. *How to Do Things with Words.* 2nd ed. Cambridge: Harvard University Press, 1962.

Bal, Mieke. *Death and Dissymmetry: The Politics of Coherence in the Book of Judges.* Chicago: University of Chicago Press, 1988.

Bales, Kevin, and Zoe Trodd, eds. *To Plead Our Own Cause: Personal Stories by Today's Slaves.* Ithaca: Cornell, 2008.

Barker, Kit. *Imprecation as Divine Discourse: Speech Act Theory, Dual Authorship and Theological Interpretation.* Journal of Theological Interpretation Supplement 16. Winona Lake: Eisenbrauns, 2016.

Beldman, David H. "The Completion of Judges: Strategies of Ending in Judges 17–21." Unpublished PhD thesis, University of Bristol, 2013.

Benjamin, Walter. *On the Concept of History Gesammelte Schriften I.2* (1974). Translated by Dennis Redmond. Accessed July 16, 2019, www.arts.yorku.ca/soci/barent/wp-content/uploads/2008/10/benjaminconcept_of_history1.pdf.

Benjamin, Walter. *The Arcades Project.* Translated by Howard Eiland and Kevin McLaughlin. Cambridge: Harvard University Press, 1999.

Block, Daniel I. "Echo Narrative Technique in Hebrew Literature: A Study in Judges 19." *Westminster Theological Journal* 52, no. 2 (1990): 325–41.

Block, Daniel I. *Judges, Ruth: New American Commentary, Volume 6.* Nashville: Broadman & Holman Publishers, 1999.

Blyth, Caroline. "Terrible Silence, Eternal Silence: A Feminist Re-reading of Dinah's Voicelessness in Genesis 34." *Biblical Interpretation* 17, no. 5 (2009): 483–506.

Bohmbach, Karla G. "Conventions/Contraventions: The Meanings of Public and Private for the Judges 19 Concubine." *Journal for the Study of the Old Testament* 24, no. 83 (1999): 83–98.

Boling, Robert G. *Judges: Introduction, Translation, and Commentary.* Anchor Bible Commentary, Vol. 6A. New Haven: Yale University Press, 2008.

Bourdieu, Pierre. *Masculine Domination.* Translated by Richard Nice. Stanford: Stanford University Press, 2001.

Brooks, Keith L. *Summarized Bible: Complete Summary of the Old Testament.* Los Angeles: Bible Institute of Los Angeles, 2009.

Brownmiller, Susan. *Against Our Will: Men, Women, and Rape.* New York: Ballantine Books, 1993.

Burney, C. F. *The Book of Judges with Introduction and Notes.* New York: KTAV Publishing House, 1918 (1970 edition).

Burt, Martha R. "Cultural Myths and Supports for Rape." *Journal of Personality and Social Psychology* 38, no. 2 (1980): 217–30.

Butler, Judith. "Foucault and the Paradox of Bodily Inscriptions." *The Journal of Philosophy* 86, no. 11 (1989): 601–7.

Butler, Judith. *Precarious Life: The Powers of Mourning and Violence.* London: Verso, 2004.

Butler, Judith. "Is Judaism Zionism?" In *The Power of Religion in the Public Sphere*, edited by Judith Butler et al., 70–91. New York: Columbia University Press, 2011.

Butler, Trent C. *Word Biblical Commentary, Volume 8: Judges.* Nashville: Word, 2009.

Cahill, Ann. "Foucault, Rape, and the Construction of the Feminine Body." *Hypatia* 15, no. 1 (2000): 43–63.

Carr, David. *The Formation of the Hebrew Bible: A New Reconstruction.* Oxford: Oxford University Press, 2011.

Claassens, Juliana. *Claiming Her Dignity: Female Resistance in the Old Testament.* Collegeville: Liturgical Press, 2016.

Clarke, Adam. *Judges.* Albany: Ages Software, 1999 (electronic edition).

Cottrill, Amy C. "A Reading of Ehud and Jael Through the Lens of Affect Theory." *Biblical Interpretation* 22, no. 4–5 (2014): 430–49.

Crenshaw, Kimberle Williams. "Demarginalizing the Intersection of Race and Sex: A Black Feminist Critique of Antidiscrimination Doctrine, Feminist Theory and Antiracist Politics." *University of Chicago Legal Forum* (1989): 139–67.

Cundall, A. E. "Judges – An Apology for the Monarchy?" *Expository Times* 81 (1969–70): 178–81.

Derrida, Jacques. *Dissemination.* Translated by Barbara Johnson. London: Continuum, 1981.

Donovan, Roxanne, and Michelle Williams. "Living at the Intersection: The Effects of Racism and Sexism on Black Rape Survivors." *Women & Therapy* 25, no. 3–4 (2002): 95–105.

Edenburg, Cynthia. *Dismembering the Whole: Composition and Purpose of Judges 19–21.* Atlanta: SBL Press, 2016.

Epstein, Louis M. "The Hebrew Family: A Study in Historical Sociology by Earle Bennett Cross (Review)." *The Jewish Quarterly Review* 20, no. 4 (1930): 367–71.

Eynikel, Erik. "Judges 19–21, an 'Appendix:' Rape, Murder, War and Abduction." *Communio Viatorum* 47 (2005): 101–15.

Exum, Cheryl. *Fragmented Women: Feminist (Sub)versions of Biblical Narratives. JSOT Suppl. 163.* Sheffield: Sheffield Academic Press, 1993.

Fewell, Danna Nolan, and David M. Gunn. *Gender, Power, and Promise: The Subject of the Bible's First Story.* Nashville: Abingdon Press, 1993.

Fortune, Marie M. "The Nature of Abuse." *Pastoral Psychology* 41, no. 5 (1993): 275–88.

Foucault, Michel. *The History of Sexuality, Volume 1.* New York: Vintage, 1980.

Foucault, Michel. *Power/Knowledge: Selected Interviews and Other Writings, 1972–1977.* Edited and translated by C. Gordon. New York: Pantheon Books, 1980.

Freytag, Ralferd C. "The Hebrew Prophets and Sodom and Gomorrah." *Consensus* 32, no. 2 (2008): 4.

Fuchs, Esther. *Sexual Politics in the Biblical Narrative: Reading the Hebrew Bible as a Woman.* London: A&C Black, 2003.

Garber, David G. Jr., and Daniel Stallings. "Awakening Desire Before It Is Season: Reading Biblical Texts in Response to the Sexual Exploitation of Children." *Review & Expositor* 105, no. 3 (2008): 453–69.

Gravett, Sandie. "Reading 'rape' in the Hebrew Bible: A Consideration of Language." *Journal for the Study of the Old Testament* 28, no. 3 (2004): 279–99.

Hackett, Jo Ann. "Violence and Women's Lives in the Book of Judges." *Interpretation* (October 2004): 356–64.

Hamley, Isabelle. "What's Wrong with 'Playing the Harlot'? The Meaning of זנה in Judges 19:2." *Tyndale Bulletin* 66, no. 1 (2015).

Harding, James. "Homophobia and Masculine Domination in Judges 19–21." *The Bible and Critical Theory* 12, no. 2 (2016): 41–74.

Hedges, Chris. *Empire of Illusion: The End of Literacy and the Triumph of Spectacle.* New York: Nation, 2009.

Henry, Matthew. *Matthew Henry's Commentary on the Whole Bible: Complete and Unabridged in One Volume.* Peabody: Hendrickson, 1994.

Hewitt, Marsha. "The Redemptive Power of Memory: Walter Benjamin and Elisabeth Schüssler Fiorenza." *Journal of Feminist Studies in Religion* 10, no. 1 (1994).

Huckin, T. "Textual Silence and the Discourse of Homelessness." *Discourse Society* 13 (2002): 347–72.

Hudson, Don Michael. "Living in a Land of Epithets: Anonymity in Judges 19–21." *Journal for the Study of the Old Testament* 19, no. 62 (1994): 49–66.

Jeffreys, Sheila. *The Industrial Vagina: The Political Economy of the Global Sex Trade.* London: Routledge, 2009.

Keefe, Alice A. "Rapes of Women, Wars of Men." *Semeia* 61 (1993): 79–97.

Knust, Jennifer. "Who's Afraid of Canaan's Curse? Genesis 9:18–29 and the Challenge of Reparative Reading." *Biblical Interpretation* 22 (2014): 388–413.

Koehler, L., W. Baumgartner, M. E. J. Richardson, and J. J. Stamm. *The Hebrew and Aramaic Lexicon of the Old Testament.* Leiden: E. J. Brill, 1994–2000.

Lasine, Stuart. "Guest and Host in Judges 19: Lot's Hospitality in an Inverted World." *Journal for the Study of the Old Testament* 29 (1984): 37–59.

Livesey, Andrea H. 'Race, Slavery, and the Expression of Sexual Violence' in *The Octoroon*, Louisa Picquet (ed.)," *American Nineteenth Century History* 19, no. 3 (2018): 267–88.

MacKinnon, Catharine A., and Andrea Dworkin. "Minneapolis Ordinance, 1983." In *In Harm's Way: The Pornography Civil Rights Hearings*, 426–31. Cambridge: Harvard University Press, 1997.

Marcos, Natalio Fernández. *Biblical Hebraica: Quinta editione cum apparatu critic novis curis elabaorato.* Stuttgart: Deutsche Bibelgesellschaft, 2011.

Matthews, V. H., and D. C. Benjamin. *Social World of Ancient Israel 1260–587.* Peabody: Hendrickson, 1993.

Miller, Jody, and Martin D. Schwartz. "Rape Myths and Violence Against Street Prostitutes." *Deviant Behavior* 16, no. 1 (1995): 1–23.

Moore, George F. *A Critical and Exegetical Commentary on Judges.* Edinburgh: T&T Clark, 1895.

Morgenstern, Julian. "Beena Marriage (Matriarchat) in Ancient Israel and its Historical Implications." *Zeitschrift für die Alttestamentliche Wissenschaft* 47, no. 1 (1929): 91–110.

Morgenstern, Julian. "Additional Notes on Beena Marriage (Matriarchat) in Ancient Israel." *Zeitschrift für die alttestamentliche Wissenschaft* 49, no. 1 (1931): 46–58.

Moster, David Z. "The Levite of Judges 19–21." *JBL* 134, no. 4 (2015): 721–30.

New King James Study Bible. Grand Rapids: Zondervan, 2018.

Niditch, Susan. *Judges: A Commentary.* Louisville: John Knox Press, 2008.

Paynter, Helen. *Reduced Laughter: Seriocomic Features and Their Functions in the Book of Kings.* Leiden: Brill, 2016.

Paynter, Helen. "Towards a Thick Description of Biblical Violence." In *Proceedings of the First Academic Symposium of the Centre for the Study of Bible and Violence*, edited by H. Paynter and M. Spalione. Sheffield: Sheffield Phoenix, forthcoming.

82   *Works consulted*

Pitts, Chuck. "Judges 19 as a Paradigm for Understanding and Responding to Human Trafficking." *Priscilla Papers* 29, no. 4 (2015): 3–6.

Polzin, Robert. *Moses and the Deuteronomist: A Literary Study of the Deuteronomic History*. New York: Seabury Press, 1980.

Poythress, Vern Sheridan. "Canon and Speech Act: Limitations in Speech-act theory, with Implications for a Putative Theory of Canonical Speech Acts." *Westminster Theological Journal* 70 (2008): 337–54.

Rabin, Chaim. "The Origin of the Hebrew Word Pileges." *Journal of Jewish Studies* 25, no. 3 (1974): 353–64.

Reinhartz, Adele. *"Why Ask My Name?" Anonymity and Identity in Biblical Narrative*. Translated by Jonathan Chipman. Oxford: Oxford University Press, 1998.

Reis, Pamela T. "The Levite's Concubine: New Light on a Dark Story." *Scandinavian Journal of the Old Testament* 20, no. 1 (2006): 125–46.

Riley, Denise. *Impersonal Passion: Language as Affect*. Durham: Duke University Press, 2005.

Robinson, Simon J. *Opening Up Judges*. Leominster: Day One Publications, 2006.

Scarry, Elaine. *The Body in Pain: The Making and Unmaking of the World*. Oxford: Oxford University Press, 1985.

Schneider, Tammi. *Judges: Berit Olam Commentary*. Collegeville: Liturgical Press, 2000.

Scholz, Susanne. *Sacred Witness: Rape in the Hebrew Bible*. Minneapolis: Fortress, 2010.

Schroeder, Joy A. *Dinah's Lament: The Biblical Legacy of Sexual Violence in Christian Interpretation*. Minneapolis: Fortress Press, 2007.

Schulte, Leah Rediger. *The Absence of God in Biblical Rape Narratives*. Philadelphia: Fortress Press, 2017.

Schüssler Fiorenza, Elisabeth. *Bread Not Stone: The Challenge of Feminist Biblical Interpretation*. Boston: Beacon Press, 1984.

Schüssler Fiorenza, Elisabeth. *In Memory of Her: A Feminist Theological Reconstruction of Christian Origins*. New York: Crossroad, 1990.

Scott, James. *Domination and the Arts of Resistance: Hidden Transcripts*. New Haven: Yale University Press, 1990.

Sedgwick, Eve Kosovsky. *Novel Gazing: Queer Readings in Fiction*. Durham: Duke University Press, 1997.

Smith, Mitzi J. "Reading the Story of the Levite's Concubine Through the Lens of Modern-Day Sex Trafficking." *Ashland Theological Journal* 41 (2009): 19–36.

Soggin, J. Alberto. *Judges, a Commentary*. Translated by John Bowden. London: SCM Press, 1981.

Southwood, Katherine. *Marriage by Capture in the Book of Judges: An Anthropological Approach*. Cambridge: Cambridge University Press, 2017.

Sternberg, Meir. *The Poetics of Biblical Narrative: Ideological Literature and the Drama of Reading*. Bloomington: Indiana University Press, 1985.

Sternberg, Meir. "Biblical Poetics and Sexual Politics: From Reading to Counterreading." *Journal of Biblical Literature* 111 (1992): 463–88.

Suzuki, Yumi. "Rape: Theories of." *The Encyclopedia of Theoretical Criminology* (2014): 703–5.

Totten, Samuel, Paul Robert Bartrop, and Steven L. Jacobs. *Dictionary of Genocide: Volume 1. ABC-CLIO*. London: Greenwood, 2008.

Tov, Emmanuel. *Textual Criticism of the Hebrew (Bible Second revised edition)*. Minneapolis: Fortress, 2001.

Trible, Phyllis. *Texts of Terror: Literary-feminist Readings of Biblical Narratives*. London: SCM Press, 1984.

Van Clief-Stefanon, Lyrae. "The Daughter and the Concubine from the Nineteenth Chapter of Judges Consider and Speak Their Minds." In *Black Swan*, Pitt Poetry Series, edited by Ed Ochester, 31–36. University of Pittsburgh Press, 2002.

Watson, Robert A. *The Book of Judges and Ruth*. Hartford: S. S. Scranton, 1903.

Webb, Barry G. *The Book of Judges, An Integrated Reading. JSOT Suppl. 46*. Sheffield: Sheffield Academic Press, 1987.

Wiegman, Robyn. "The Times We're in: Queer Feminist Criticism and the Reparative 'Turn'." *Feminist Theory* 15, no. 1 (2014): 4–25.

Wilcock, Michael. *The Message of Judges: Grace Abounding. The Bible Speaks Today*. Nottingham: Inter-Varsity Press, 1992.

Yoo, Yani. "Han-laden Women: Korean "Comfort Women" and Women in Judges 19–21." *Semeia* 78 (1997): 37.

Index

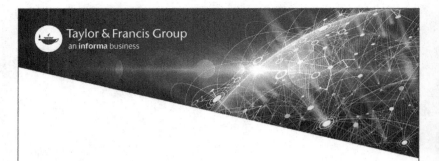

Printed in the United States
by Baker & Taylor Publisher Services